STUDIES IN THE (

CW00376187

Supply side economics

Second edition

Nigel Healey
University of Leicester
and
Rosalind Levačić
Open University

Series Editor
Bryan Hurl

HEINEMANN
EDUCATIONAL

Heinemann Educational,
a division of Heinemann Publishers (Oxford) Ltd.
Halley Court, Jordan Hill, Oxford OX2 8EJ

OXFORD   LONDON   EDINBURGH
MADRID   ATHENS   BOLOGNA   PARIS
MELBOURNE   SYDNEY   AUCKLAND   SINGAPORE   TOKYO
IBADAN   NAIROBI   HARARE   GABORONE
PORTSMOUTH NH (USA)

© Nigel Healey and Rosalind Levačić, 1988, 1992

First published 1988

Second Edition 1992

93 94 95 96 10 9 8 7 6 5 4 3 2

British Library Cataloguing in Publication Data

A catalogue record for this book is available from the British Library

ISBN 0 435 33020 9

Typeset and illustrated by Taurus Graphics, Kidlington, Oxon.

Printed and bound in Great Britain by **Loader Jackson**, Arlesey.

Acknowledgements

The authors are grateful to Bryan Hurl for his editing of the final version of the book and
to Celine Noronha for typing the original maunscript.

The Publishers would like to thank the following for permission to reproduce copyright
material:

Associated Examining Board for the questions on pp. 18, 35, 45, 60, 75 and 88; the
Central Statistical Office for the table on p. 15; the *Economist* for the articles on
pp. 30–31 and 50; the *Guardian* for the article by Nick Crafts on pp. 12–13; the
Independent on Sunday for the article by Peter Clarke on pp. 42–43; Joint Matriculation
Board for the questions on pp. 18, 35, 60, 74 and 85; Rachelle Maxwell for the two
cartoons on pp. 6 and 51; the OECD for the tables on pp. 12, 15 and 32–33; Oxford &
Cambridge Schools Examination Board for the questions on pp. 18, 35, 45, 60, 74 and
85–86; University of Cambridge Local Examinations Syndicate for the question on p. 36;
University of London Examinations Assessment Council for the questions on pp. 18, 35,
45, 60, 74, 75, 85 and 88; University of Oxford Delegacy of local Examinations for the
questions on pp. 18, 45, 60 and 85; Welsh Joint Education Committee for the question
on p. 75;

The publishers have made every effort to contact the correct copyright holders. However,
if any material has been incorrectly acknowledged, the Publishers will be pleased to make
the necessary arrangements at the earliest opportunity.

ii

Contents

Preface to Second Edition

This series aims to appeal to schools and colleges where both teachers and those taught are eager to get to grips with the real economy of the UK. *Supply Side Economics* applies micro and macro theory in an up-to-date way.

Traditional textbooks still give full coverage to the over-simple Keynesian diagrams universally taught in the 1960s. But the post-Keynesian world makes the inverted L-shaped aggregate demand curve look increasingly unrealistic. The world has changed and so has the quality of economic analysis. Unfortunately the response of textbooks has been very lagged indeed!

As a compliment to the first edition of this book – and its success – new textbooks and revisions of their older predecessors now include an obligatory chapter on 'supply side economics'. On the face of it this should offer healthy competition in a deregulated market – but Nigel Healey has rewritten and reordered this important text so that the second edition is still in the vanguard.

Bryan Hurl
Series Editor

Introduction

'What happens to the supply side will, in the long run, be the main determinant of our economic success.' Nigel Lawson

The term 'supply side economics' was first coined in 1976 by Herbert Stein, a professor at the University of Virginia, to describe economic policies designed to influence output and employment through their impact on the supply side, as opposed to the demand side, of the economy. Although the term is relatively new, however, the basic concept is not. Ever since 1945, governments of varying political persuasions have attempted to strengthen the supply side in their quests for more rapid economic growth. In the mid-1960s, for example, Mr Wilson's Labour government came to power pledged to restructure and rationalize British industry and thereby induce growth rates of five per cent a year. Mr Heath's Conservative government similarly took office in 1970 on a promise to revitalize the supply side and so end Britain's relative economic decline.

Until 1979, however, supply side policy took second place to demand management. While successive governments recognized the potential benefits of directly promoting the supply side of the economy, it was generally believed that the major contribution governments could make to economic prosperity was to keep – through the active use of demand management – the economy as close as possible to 'full-employment'. By ensuring that aggregate demand was always high enough to allow firms to work at full capacity, it was argued, governments could create a stable, supportive economic environment in which firms had the confidence and incentive to invest for growth.

In the period 1945–79, supply side policy thus played an essentially supporting role, with governments intervening directly in the supply side in areas where a high and stable level of aggregate demand did not, of itself, appear to be sufficient to stimulate investment and growth. Such measures often involved prodding laggardly firms into action, normally by offering them additional financial incentives to invest (e.g. tax allowances or cash grants). In extreme cases, the government might nationalize private companies, in order to ensure that socially desirable

1

investment in new plant and equipment was undertaken. In the 1970s, for example, companies like Rolls–Royce and Rover (then British Leyland) were taken into public ownership and restructured with tax-payers' money, after their original managements had failed to maintain their international competitiveness.

Underpinning both demand management and supply side policies during the so-called 'Keynesian era' was a deep-seated distrust of the free market and a feeling that the 'invisible hand' was unable to coordinate economic activity and achieve growth. Without the active involvement of paternalistic government, it was concluded, it would be impossible to achieve economic success. Demand management was considered so important because it was felt that, in the absence of compensating adjustments in monetary and fiscal policy, the level of aggregate demand would tend to fluctuate wildly, rarely reaching the level necessary for full employment. Similarly, supply side policy took the form of intervening in the decision-making of the private sector, on the grounds that such decisions would otherwise be irrational and shortsighted.

This pessimistic view of free markets was successfully challenged by the *new classical economists* in the late 1970s, who provided the intellectual inspiration for the economic policies that have been pursued since 1979. The new classical economists reasserted the power of free markets to deliver economic prosperity, denying that governments could systematically increase output and employment through the use of either demand-management or interventionist supply side policies. They argued that demand management ultimately resulted in inflation, concluding that it was futile and misguided. More radically still, they rejected Keynesian notions of *market failure*, claiming that the best way to strengthen the supply side was not via direct government intervention but rather by cutting taxes and liberating otherwise vital market forces from cloying state bureaucracy.

Although Keynesians and new classical economists remain sharply divided over the appropriate role of government in the economy, *both schools of thought agree that the subject matter of 'supply side economics' is the economics of growth*. Supply side economics focuses on the reasons why some countries are rich and some are poor.

- Why is it, for example, that Czechoslovakia, once the fifth most powerful industrial power in the world, has now fallen behind most of South East Asia in terms of per capita income?
- Why does the USA, for almost a century the most powerful economic nation on earth, now buy half its cars from Japan and rely on borrowing from overseas to pay for its imports?

- How have Singapore and South Korea transformed impoverished, resource-scarce countries into affluent, export-oriented economies?

Although this book does not answer all these questions directly, it examines the most important reasons why the UK has fallen behind in the 'growth race' and considers the policies that have been deployed in recent years in an attempt to stem Britain's relative economic decline.

Chapter 1 examines Britain's supply side performance, both relative to historical trends and in comparison with our major trading partners.

Chapter 2 explores the determinants of economic growth, highlighting the role of training and education, capital investment and technological progress.

Chapter 3 reviews traditional, Keynesian approaches to supply side policy, which were predicated on the assumption that slow growth was due to market failure.

Chapter 4 outlines the new classical backlash of the 1980s and 90s, in which privatization, deregulation and market liberalization were prescribed as the key elements of supply side revival.

Chapters 5 and 6 then appraise the performance of recent supply side policy in the key areas of tax reform, social security and labour market reform.

Finally, we offer some insights into the likely evolution of supply side policy for the rest of this century.

Reading list

Harrison, B., Smith, C. and Davies, B., Chapter 37 in *Introductory Economics*, Macmillan, 1992.

Levačić, R., 'What is supply side economics?', *Economic Review*, 1988, vol. 6(1), pp. 7–12.

Powell, R., Chapter 23 in *Economics A-Level Course Companion*, Letts, 1991.

Chapter One

The UK's supply side performance

'Other countries have far greater problems than we have.'
Sir Edward Heath

Introduction

Politicians and economists often talk about the 'supply side' of the economy. Ministers claim that their policies are designed to 'strengthen the supply side'. Economists refer to improvements or emerging weaknesses in the 'supply side' performance of the economy. Implicit in such statements is the idea that the *'supply side' relates to Britain's basic economic competitiveness*; that is, the country's ability to produce goods and services that consumers want, at a price they are prepared to pay.

The simplest way to express the same basic notion in more familiar, textbook terms is to think of a simple aggregate supply and demand diagram (see Figure 1). The aggregate supply (AS) schedule shows how much firms in the economy will produce at different price levels, while the aggregate demand (AD) schedule shows the quantities of output that the nation as a whole (households, businesses and government taken together) want to buy at different price levels. *The 'supply side', therefore, is the part of the economy which lies behind the AS schedule*; that is, the companies and workers engaged in the production of goods and services.

From year to year, AD fluctuates up and down, often causing quite sharp changes in total output which are independent of developments on the supply side. But, in the long run, it is more fundamental changes on the supply side of the economy (e.g. new products and processes, better educated workers, more efficient plant and equipment) that allow economies to enjoy ever-higher levels of output. Bitter experience has taught us that, if pumping up demand through higher government spending and rapid credit creation were the route to lasting economic prosperity, the UK would be one of the richest countries in the developed world. But Table 1 shows that the UK has fallen steadily from its ranking as the richest country in Europe to below average in the European Community.

Within the context of the AS–AD model in Figure 1, *underlying*

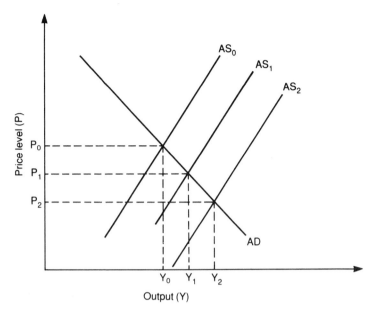

Figure 1 Basic aggregate supply and demand model

improvements in the supply side manifest themselves as a continuous, rightward shift in the AS schedule over time (e.g. from AS_0 to AS_1 to AS_2), steadily increasing the quantity of output that firms supply at any given level of AD.

Table 1 Per capita GDP (as a percentage of the EC average)

Country	1960	1992
Japan	44.7	148.1
Denmark	123.2	132.1
Germany	123.8	129.2
Luxembourg	158.0	126.2
USA	268.7	117.7
France	126.9	109.0
Belgium	115.4	103.4
Italy	75.2	104.2
Netherlands	97.0	97.4
UK	131.1	94.1

Source: *European Economy*

Somewhat confusingly, when professional economists speak of 'economic growth', they often mean nothing more than the change in output over a relatively short period (e.g. one year). We read newspaper reports along the following lines: 'The Treasury today forecast 2 per cent growth over the next twelve months'; or 'The opposition leader again declared that, owing to the government's mishandling of the economy, Britain will suffer the slowest growth of any major industrial country this year.' However, as Figure 2 suggests, changes in output over such short periods are driven primarily by fluctuations in AD (e.g. from AD_0 to AD_1 to AD_2). In 1991, output in the UK fell by 2.1 per cent as a slump in consumption and investment spending pushed the economy into a deep recession. Only three years earlier, in contrast, buoyant demand had boosted output by 4.7 per cent.

Yet in neither case did the actual changes in output reflect what was happening to the country's underlying supply side capacity. The 'growth' experienced in 1988 was largely achieved by using the nation's existing capital stock and workforce more intensively. During 1988, surveys by the Confederation of British Industry (CBI) showed a marked increase in the percentage of companies reporting that they were producing at full capacity, while registered unemployment dropped rapidly. In 1991, on the other hand, many firms were working

"If I'm 20% better off in real terms than I was in 1979, why am I broke?"

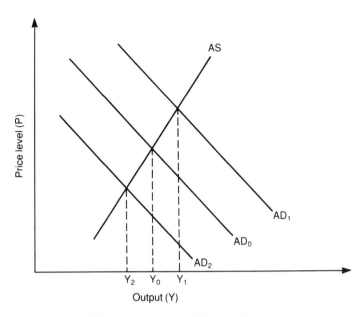

Figure 2 The effect on output of fluctuations in aggregate demand

far below capacity. They ran fewer shifts, putting some staff on short-time working and laying-off those for whom they had insufficient work. Unemployment rose accordingly.

Output and unemployment

Figure 3 illustrates diagrammatically the cyclical pattern that the economy tends to follow. The broken line represents actual output, while the solid line shows the underlying, long-run growth in the economy's productive capacity. It is this **natural rate of output**, rather than the actual year-to-year level, which is influenced by changes in the supply side.

During boom years, when the growth of output is accelerating above its natural rate, unemployment falls steadily and actual output is driven above the natural rate of output. Companies have to work nearer to full capacity; bottlenecks appear in the economy; unemployment drops and firms suffer labour shortages, leading them to bid up wage levels; inflation accelerates.

Once the boom has peaked and the economy moves into recession, the growth in output slumps below that of the natural rate, possibly even becoming negative, as in 1980–81 and 1990–91. Unemployment mounts, as many firms lay off unneeded workers; others go out of business altogether; inflation slows.

7

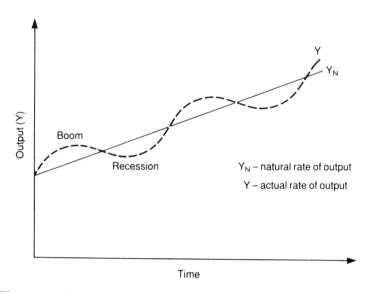

Figure 3 The cyclical nature of the economy

This account of the **stop–go**, 'boom-bust' cycles followed by market economies underscores the key relationship on the supply side of the economy between output and unemployment. It should be evident that *rising output, of itself, does not signal an improvement in the supply side of the economy.* Any country, provided that it first undergoes a deep recession, can temporarily enjoy a period of 'economic growth', simply by allowing an expansion in AD to mop up underutilized resources and temporarily propel actual output above its natural rate – whether or not that natural rate of output has in fact increased. During the 1980s, for example, the Conservative government talked enthusiastically about the 'supply side miracle' induced by its policies, citing as evidence the rapid rate of economic growth (i.e. the average, year-on-year growth of real output) between 1981 and 1989.

The Labour opposition replied that the increased rate of economic growth reflected nothing more than the severity of the 1979–81 recession, with actual output having to grow faster than the natural rate of output over the period 1981–89 to make up for the ground lost at the beginning of the decade. By stripping out the effects of the economic cycle, critics of the Conservative government argued – for example, by measuring the average growth of output from peak-to-peak (or trough-to-trough) – that it could be shown that the underlying, long-run growth of output had changed little between the 1970s and the 1980s. Conservative ministers responded that the growth rates enjoyed in the period 1981–89 constituted a once-for-all 'jump' to a new, higher underlying growth rate, which would be restored as soon as the economy recovered from the recession of the early 1990s.

Whatever the truth of the matter, the message is clear. In terms of the supply side of the economy, what matters is the growth of the natural rate of output; that is, the long-run rate of economic growth that can be sustained over time. Short-run fluctuations in the growth of actual output, which are mirrored by changes in unemployment – with unemployment falling at times of above-average economic growth and vice versa – tell us very little about changes in the fundamental strength of the supply side.

Labour productivity

A composite guide to the vitality of the supply side is the rate of growth of **labour productivity**. Labour productivity measures the output per worker – that is, total output divided by total employment. We know that output can be increased by reducing unemployment, but unless productivity is also raised, such gains do not indicate any sustainable improvement in the supply side of the economy. Output per head, therefore, offers a guide to the performance of the supply side, by effectively 'adjusting' increases in output for any change in the level of unemployment.

Although labour productivity gives a better picture of the trends in the underlying developments in the supply side, its behaviour is, unfortunately, also sensitive to the effects of the economic cycle. In the early stages of a **recession**, firms may be unsure how long the downturn will last and typically 'hoard' their best workers, choosing to cut output and temporarily pay staff in excess of their marginal revenue product in order to avoid the costs of firing and subsequently rehiring workers when business picks up. As a result, output growth falls, but unemployment initially rises only slightly, so that the early stages of the downturn are characterized by a slowdown in productivity growth. At the **trough** of the recession, however, firms are forced to reassess their prospects and lay off workers in order to cut costs. In the middle stages of the recession, therefore, while output growth may not slow any further, unemployment will begin to rise rapidly and the productivity of those employees that remain in work rises.

As **recovery** begins to gather pace, firms expand output by using their existing workforces more intensively – for example, by working staff overtime – waiting to be sure that the upturn will be sustained. Output growth accordingly picks up; but, with unemployment little affected, productivity growth accelerates further. Only once the recovery is in full swing and firms start taking on additional staff does unemployment begin to fall. As the economy approaches the peak of the boom, productivity growth gradually slows. Figure 4 illustrates the course of output, unemployment and productivity over the four stages of the economic cycle: recession, trough, recovery and peak.

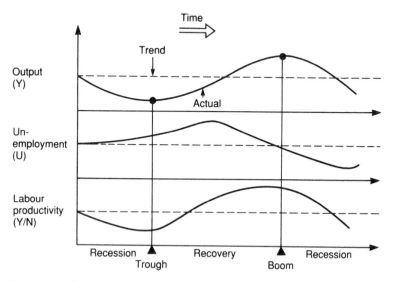

Figure 4 The courses of output, unemployment and labour productivity

Since **unemployment** is simply the difference between the potential labour force and employment, we can highlight the triangular nature of the relationship between output, employment and labour productivity.

Productivity = Output/Employment
Output = Productivity × Employment
Output growth (%) = Productivity growth + Employment growth (%)

If the potential labour force is unchanged over time (as it is in many European economies, in which the population is fairly static), then in the long run the growth in labour productivity will be equal to output growth. But in the short run, when employment can fluctuate greatly, output growth can give a misleading impression of the underlying changes in the supply side, as reflected in changes in productivity. This trinity also illustrates why, in the recovery phase of the economic cycle when productivity normally grows most quickly, unemployment can continue to rise even though output is growing: unless output growth is as least as fast as the growth in productivity, the extra output can be produced with ever fewer workers.

The UK's supply side performance

We can now turn to consider the UK's supply side performance. Table 2 sets out the performance of the British supply side over the last 30 years. It shows that, following a period of unprecedented economic growth in the period 1963–73 – when output (real GDP) grew more rapidly than at any time since the industrial revolution – the rate of economic growth slowed sharply. The so-called 'long boom' of the 1960s and early 1970s was punctured by the first OPEC oil crisis, when oil prices quadrupled, tipping the world – and the UK – into a deep recession. Since then, while growth has picked up slightly during the period 1979–92, the improvement is marginal.

Table 2 Performance of the British supply side, 1963–92 (% average annual change, year-on-year)

Years (annual average)	Real GDP	Manufacturing output	Labour productivity	Employment	Gross fixed investment
1963–73	3.3	3.6	2.9	0.2	4.8
1973–79	1.5	0.5	1.1	0.2	0.3
1979–92 (est.)	1.8	0.6	1.8	0.1	2.1

Source: Goldman Sachs

The picture for the economy as a whole is even worse for the manufacturing sector. Although structural change now means that manufacturing constitutes only about 20 per cent of total GDP (services account for 70 per cent of total output), it continues to generate over half of the UK's export revenues and the vitality of the manufacturing sector is crucial to the nation's economic success – as Germany and Japan have graphically illustrated. Many economists believe that the sluggish growth of manufacturing output, which by 1992 was only marginally above 1973 levels, poses grave long-term problems for the British economy. As North Sea oil revenues dwindle, they argue, Britain's consumers will be unable to enjoy the CD players, VCRs and high-tech cars that Japanese and German exporters presently supply, but which domestic companies no longer produce.

Renewed role for government as UK seeks to close productivity gap

Nick Crafts

Two or three years ago there was widespread optimism that Britain was on the threshold of a real break-through in productivity which would see the economy catch up, or even overtake, continental Europe and would permit rapid increases in wages to co-exist with stable prices. Now assessments have turned gloomy as high inflation has returned and productivity growth has noticeably slowed.

This prompts three questions. First, how good was performance in the 1980s? Second, how successful have the policy reforms of the Thatcher years been? Third, what does analysis of the recent past suggest about future prospects?

The productivity performance of the 1980s needs to be considered in context. Two important points are obvious from the table and the chart, namely that the improvement in relative UK performance arises from declining productivity growth elsewhere and that annual rates of growth vary with the business cycle.

The general slowdown in OECD productivity growth owes a good deal to the exhaustion of the rapid advance based on catching-up US technology and organisation.

There was a revival of British performances from the dismal 1970s level, and by the late eighties our productivity relative to that of West Germany was probably back to the position of the early 1970s. Exact measurement is difficult but, for example, Van Ark's recent estimates of output per person-hour in manufacturing show a West German lead of 5 per cent in 1960, rising to 33 per cent in 1973 and 63 per cent in 1979 but falling to 38 per cent by 1989.

The main components of the Government's attempts to reform the British supply side are well known. Important policy developments initially included lowering personal taxation, trade union legislation, deregulation, privatisation, and harsher treatment of lame ducks. More recently attention has been given to reforms of training. In addition, at an early stage, the Government signalled its willingness to allow unemployment to rise, its acceptance of a high pound and a desire to escape from the constraints on policy imposed by attempts at social contracts with trade unions. This can be seen as a repudiation of the postwar settlement, Butskellite policies and corporatism, all of which, in the Thatcher view, had been fundamental to the persistence of obstacles to higher productivity.

It should also be recognised as very different from the normal response to a recession: competitive pressures on business were deliberately increased rather than reduced. In the 1930s, for instance, in the wake of a recession, the UK encouraged cartelisation, raised tariffs, curtailed foreign lending and devalued the pound.

The outcome of the "Thatcher Experiment" was a productivity surge that owed little to greater investment but came primarily from reductions in "X-inefficiency" (rationalisation of plant, fewer restrictive practices, increased intensity of work etc).

Research at the London School of Economics identi-

Labour productivity growth in the business sector
(% per year)

	1960 –73	1973 –9	1979 –89
Japan	8.5	3.0	3.2
France	5.4	3.0	2.6
UK	3.6	1.5	2.4
Belgium	3.3	2.8	2.3
Sweden	4.1	1.5	1.8
Denmark	4.3	2.6	1.7
Italy	6.3	3.0	1.6
Netherlands	4.8	2.7	1.6
Germany	4.5	3.1	1.6
US	2.2	0.0	0.8

Source: OECD Economic Outlook, June 1990

Growth of output per person employed
(% per year)

Source: Economic Trends & Dept of Employment Gazette

fies big effects from reductions in organisational changes in the context of rising unemployment, greater competitive pressures and import penetration. Similarly research at the London Business School has documented large improvements in some nationalised industries where inefficiency was squeezed out as managers responded to a new structure of incentives. These productivity gains would surely not have been attainable under the Labour Party of the early 1980s.

On the other hand, the National Institute of Economic and Social Research has demonstrated that British standards of workforce training have fallen further behind those in other countries.

The Institute for Fiscal Studies has found, at most, a very modest impact through incentives for lowered personal taxation, and the Science Policy Research Unit has drawn attention to a relative decline in technological prowess. In these areas reliance on market forces and an attack on "X-inefficiency" are less relevant.

On occasions this programme for better productivity reinforced counter-inflation policy but also sometimes undermined it. The shock of rapidly rising unemployment reduced inflationary pressures and trade union restrictive practices in the early 1980s. By contrast, deregulation of capital markets and Mr Lawson's insistence on using fiscal policy to raise incentives may have been good for efficiency but led to excessive growth demand in the late 1980s.

This analysis has a number of implications. First, cyclical considerations mean that it is likely productivity growth will revive in the early 1990s, but the once-for-all nature of a good part of the 1980s productivity surge suggests it is unlikely to regain the levels of 1982/3.

Second, there is still a long way to go to achieve the levels of productivity elsewhere in the OECD. This potential for catch-up may well favour our relative productivity growth performance but our weaknesses in labour force skills can be expected to prevent an early closing of the productivity gap.

Third, in areas like training there is an important role for government policy to reduce the extent of market failures. If the Conservatives win the election, they would be wise to take this point more seriously.

Fourth, productivity outcomes seem to depend significantly on factors such as the credibility of governmental regulatory policies, the exposure of managers to competition and the state of the labour market. Should Labour win the election, it will be important for it to design policy accordingly.

Nick Crafts is Professor of Economic History at the University of Warwick and Co-Director of the Human Resources Since 1900 Programme, Centre for Economic Policy Research.

Source: *The Guardian*, 5 December 1990

Labour productivity growth has also fallen sharply since the long boom. Although the period of 1973–79 recorded a dismal annual 1.1 per cent growth in productivity, the improvement since then has been patchy. In the mid-1980s, productivity rattled along at well above 3 per cent a year, encouraging some commentators to conclude that the 1970s had been a temporary departure from long-term trends. But once the recessions of 1980–81 and 1990–91 are taken into account, the underlying trend for the period 1979–92 is rather more worrying.

Interestingly, Table 2 shows that employment has grown slowly, but steadily, over the last 30 years. This apparently contradicts the widespread impression that unemployment has been on a relentless upward trend since the mid-1960s. In fact, a combination of demographic and social trends has meant that both rising employment *and* unemployment have occurred simultaneously (see Figure 5). While the underlying demand for labour has been continuously expanding, at the same time the supply of labour has grown even more rapidly: more and more young mothers now work; structural changes in working patterns mean that women who would previously have been forced to stay at home can work part-time; 'bulges' in the birth rate during the 1960s fed through to cause a temporary 'blip' in the size of the labour force during the 1980s (although this has begun to reverse in recent years).

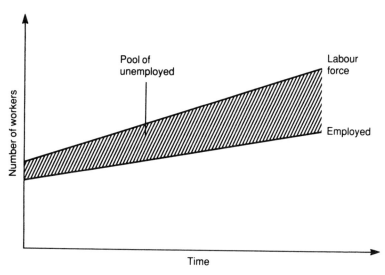

Figure 5 Graphical demonstration that employment and unemployment rises can occur simultaneously

Finally, the growth in investment has slowed over the last 30 years, although – after virtual stagnation during the period 1973–79 – it actually grew rather more rapidly than output (implying that the proportion of GDP invested has risen) between 1979 and 1992. Nevertheless, although the UK enjoyed something of an investment boom during the late 1980s, the increase in the total capital stock since 1979 is disappointingly small. Indeed, in sectors like transport, the capital stock has actually shrunk, rather than increased, over the last 13 years.

International comparisons

In 1970, labour productivity in Britain was equal to that of Germany and almost 50 per cent higher than that of Japan (although only half that of the USA). Over the intervening period, German productivity has inexorably accelerated away from British rates, while we have been steadily overhauled by Japan (see Figure 6). If present trends continue, per capita GDP in the UK will be overtaken by **newly industrializing countries** like South Korea, Taiwan and Singapore before the end of the century.

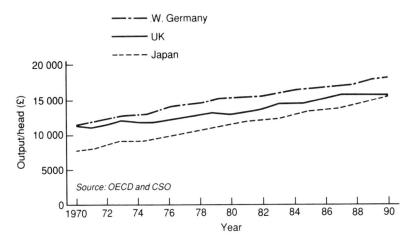

Figure 6 Comparative outputs per person (1985 sterling purchasing power parities)

It is often argued that the UK, having industrialized first, has necessarily enjoyed lower growth rates than other countries. There is some substance in this argument, but there is no systematic relationship between per capita GDP and economic growth. While once-poor countries like Singapore have enjoyed growth rates that quickly raised their living standards to European levels, countries like Guyana that were equally poor in 1960 have marked time. Similarly, rich countries like Venezuela – which boasted living standards equal to those in Germany and the UK in 1960 – have stagnated, sliding back into relative poverty. In general, there appears to be almost no relation between per capita income and rates of economic growth.

Table 3 compares the UK's supply side performance since the end of the long boom with our main partners in the European Community. It shows that on every indicator, the UK ranks last amongst the 'big four':

- GDP and labour productivity growth rates have been slower.
- Relative **unit labour costs** (see page 16) have increased more rapidly.
- Employment growth has been more sluggish.
- Gross domestic fixed capital formation has grown more slowly.

Although some of the differences appear small, it is important to bear in mind the effect of compounding. For example, over the 19 years

15

1974–92, the extra 0.5 per cent GDP growth enjoyed by France means that, had the UK and France had the same GDP in 1973, French GDP would now be over 10 per cent higher. (In fact, French GDP was already well above British GDP in 1973, so the gap now is even greater.)

Table 3 Relative performance of the British supply side, 1974–92 (% average annual changes year-on-year)

	Real GDP	Labour productivity	Relative unit labour costs*	Employment	Gross fixed Invest-ment
UK	1.8	1.6	1.7	0.1	1.2
Germany	2.2	1.8	−1.1	0.5	1.9
France	2.3	2.1	−0.5	0.2	1.4
Italy	2.8	1.9	1.5	0.9	1.6

*Relative to other EC member states
Source: *European Economy*

A note on unit labour costs

Unit labour costs are: $$\frac{\text{Wage + non-wage costs per worker}}{\text{Average product per worker}}$$

Unit labour costs therefore rise when wage or non-wage costs (e.g. employers' National Insurance contributions) increase and fall as productivity rises.

Relative unit labour costs (RULCs) are unit labour costs expressed in a common currency and related to the average of a group of countries (in Table 2, the EC as a whole). A rise in RULCs implies deteriorating competitiveness, which could stem from: a relative increase in wage or non-wage costs, in domestic currency terms; a relative decline in the growth of labour productivity; or an appreciation in the exchange rate. Conversely, a fall in RULCs implies increasing competitiveness.

Conclusions

Supply side performance is often taken to be synonymous with economic growth – that is, the rate of change of output. In fact, the rate of growth of output is highly cyclical, typically accelerating during an economic upswing and slowing during recession. It can therefore be misleading to infer what is happening to the underlying rate of economic growth from the rate of change of output over a relatively short period. Measuring output growth from peak to peak (i.e. from the peak of one cycle to the peak of the next) gives a better impression of trends on the supply side; but since no two economic cycles are precisely the same, even this approach has important limitations.

Bearing these caveats in mind, over the long run, the UK's supply side performance has been relatively poor. While output has grown at an average annual rate of approximately 2 per cent over the last 30 years, approximately doubling real living standards over this period, in comparison with other developed countries the UK has fared badly. Second only to the USA in terms of per capita income in 1960, Britain has steadily slipped down the international league table, as Japan and almost all the northern European states have overtaken us. It is to a better understanding of the reasons for the UK's poor supply side record that the next chapter turns.

KEY WORDS

Natural rate of output	Recovery
Stop–go	Peak
Labour productivity	Unemployment
Recession	Newly industralizing countries
Trough	Unit labour costs

Reading list

Bazen, S. and Thirlwall, T., *Deindustrialization*, 2nd edn, Heinemann Educational, 1992.

Blackaby, D. and Lester, L., 'An assessment of the UK's productivity record in the 1980s: has there been a "miracle"?' in Healey, N. (ed), *Britain's Economic Miracle: Myth or Reality*, Routledge, 1992.

Feinstein, C., 'Britain's economic growth: international and historical perspectives', *Economic Review*, 1990, vol. 7 (5), pp. 19–23.

Maunder, P. et al., Chapters 14 and 18 in *Economics Explained*, Collins Educational, 1991.

Paisley, R. and Quillfeldt, J., Module 14 in *Economics Investigated*, vol 2, Collins Educational, 1992.

Essay topics

1. Distinguish between the cost of living and the standard of living. Examine the factors likely to improve the standard of living in the UK. (University of London Examinations and Assessment Council, 1992)
2. Explain whether or not you regard a high growth rate as a desirable economic objective. Discuss the implications of growth for: (a) Britain and Europe; (b) the less developed world. (Joint Matriculation Board, 1991)
3. Use the concepts of aggregate demand and supply to analyse the effects of an increase in exports on output, employment and inflation. (University of Oxford Delegacy of Local Examinations, 1990)
4. 'Although many economists agree that the most important problems facing the UK economy lie on the "supply side" of the economy, there is much less agreement about the policies appropriate to deal with these problems.' What are the 'supply side' problems facing the economy, and why is there disagreement about the appropriate policies? (Associated Examining Board, 1989)

Data Response Question 1

Changes in UK international cost competitiveness in manufacturing
This task is based on a question set by the Oxford & Cambridge Schools Examination Board in 1989. Study the chart and answer the following questions.

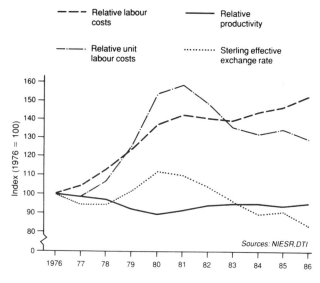

1. Define (i) relative labour costs; (ii) relative productivity; (iii) sterling effective exchange rate; (iv) relative unit labour costs.
2. Explain the difference between labour costs and wage (or salary) costs.
3. Account for the trend in relative productivity between 1976 and 1980. Does the chart confirm the view that there has been a 'productivity miracle' in the UK since 1980?
4. What factors influencing the competitiveness of the UK economy are *not* included in the chart?
5. What are the implications for the British economy of trends since 1981 in relative unit labour costs?

Chapter Two

The determinants of economic growth

'During 30 years we have tried to force the pace of growth. Growth is welcome, but we just do not know how to force its pace. Perhaps faster growth, like happiness, should not be a prime target, but a byproduct of other policies.' Sir Keith Joseph

As we saw in the previous chapter, we can think of economic growth as a continuous rightwards shift in the aggregate supply schedule in the familiar aggregate supply and demand (AS–AD) model. In considering the determinants of economic growth, a convenient starting point is therefore to consider *the factors which determine the precise position of the aggregate supply (AS) schedule at any moment in time and, by implication, the forces that could cause it to shift to the right.*

The aggregate production function

The AS schedule traces out the relationship between the average price level (P) and the quantity of real output (Y) supplied by firms in the economy. In deriving the AS schedule, we must first consider the **aggregate production function** (APF). In the short run, we assume that all factors of production except labour are fixed; that is, we assume that the state of technology is given. On this basis, we can draw the APF shown in Figure 7. It shows that the **law of diminishing returns** applies. With all other factors of production fixed, as firms employ more and more labour, real output rises, but at a diminishing rate. In other words, as firms expand employment, the marginal product of labour decreases.

The labour market

How much labour will it be profitable for all firms to employ? To answer this question, we must move to the labour market itself. Basic microeconomics teaches us that profit-maximizing firms hire labour up to the point where the last worker adds as much to total costs (i.e. the wage paid) as he or she adds to the firm's total revenue. The extra revenue generated is known as the **marginal revenue product** (MRP). Assuming perfectly competitive goods markets, MRP is simply the price of the product multiplied by marginal product (i.e. the increase to

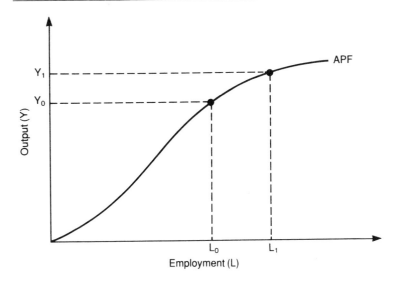

Figure 7 Aggregate production function

real output contributed by the last worker). We know from our discussion of the shape of the APF that marginal product declines as employment increases. For a given set of product prices, we can therefore derive the demand for labour schedule in Figure 8, which is simply the downward-sloping MRP schedule for the economy as a whole. It shows that as the (money) wage falls, firms in aggregate will find it profitable to employ more workers. What about the supply of labour? All other things equal, the higher the wage, the greater the amount of labour offered. The labour supply schedule is thus upward-sloping in the normal way at L_S.

We can see that, assuming that the labour market is perfectly competitive, employment and wages will be determined in the normal way by the intersection of the labour supply and demand schedules. In other words, for a given set of product prices, a fixed stock of land and capital, and labour's relative preferences for work and leisure (which determine the shape and position of the labour supply schedule), we can work out the equilibrium wage rate W_0 and level of employment L_0. Moreover, by going back to the APF in Figure 7, we can also read off the level of real output Y_0, consistent with equilibrium in the labour market.

The short-run aggregate supply schedule

To derive the AS schedule, we must now examine what happens to employment and output if prices in the economy rise. Let us suppose

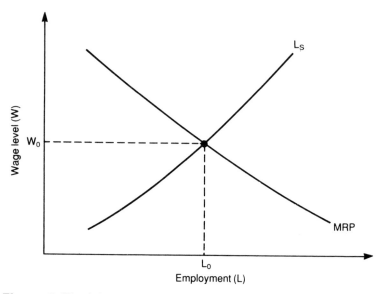

Figure 8 The labour market (see text)

that the original price level is P_0 and that prices rise to P_1. How does this affect the labour market presented in Figure 9? Consider first the situation of firms when the price level changes. Firms profit-maximize by altering employment until the money wage is equal to MRP. Each firm, in turn, calculates MRP by referring to the price of its own product, which it knows day-by-day. Thus, a 10 per cent rise in the price level, which increases all individual product prices by 10 per cent, increases each firm's MRP at any given level of employment by 10 per cent. Each firm can see the increase as soon as it takes place and adjusts its level of employment immediately. The MRP schedule in Figure 9 shifts to the right from MRP(P_0) to MRP(P_1).

Now let us look at the situation from the point of view of individual workers. We have seen that the labour supply schedule (in terms of money wages) depends on the price level. All other things equal, a 10 per cent rise in prices will cause workers to require 10 per cent higher money wages for any given number of hours of work. But the price with which workers are concerned is not the price of an individual product, but the price of all goods and services in the economy. This information is only available with a time lag and, as some prices (e.g. fruit and vegetables) fluctuate month by month owing to seasonal effects, it may take some time before a clear change in average prices becomes apparent.

What this means is that while firms respond instantaneously to a change in average prices, it may be some time before workers fully appreciate what has happened to the price level. In the intervening period they suffer **money illusion**, unable to appreciate that the value of money has changed and accordingly selling their labour at too high or too low a money wage. In Figure 9, because workers fail to appreciate that prices have risen in the short run, they supply exactly the same amount of labour as before at any given money wage; that is, the labour supply schedule remains at $L_S(P_0)$.

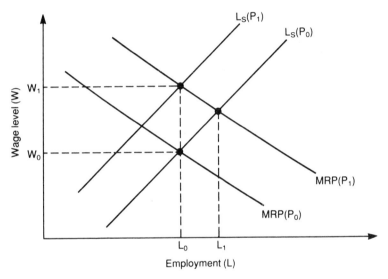

Figure 9 Illustrating money illusion

The result is that, so long as money illusion persists, the effect of the rise in prices is to shift the demand for labour to the right from $MRP(P_0)$ to $MRP(P_1)$, while leaving the supply of labour unchanged at $L_S(P_0)$. Employment increases to L_1 and, by checking with our APF in Figure 7, we can see that the effect of the price rise is to increase real output to Y_1. In the short run, therefore, while money illusion persists, workers are effectively tricked into working harder for lower **real wages** (i.e. the money wage adjusted for the effect of the rise in prices). The AS is upward-sloping (see Figure 10). When prices rise from P_0 to P_1, real output increases from Y_0 to Y_1. And because the process is completely symmetrical, when prices fall from P_0 to P_2, real output falls below Y_0.

The long-run aggregate supply schedule

Gradually, workers come to realize that prices have changed, reducing the purchasing power of the wages they receive. We must therefore label the AS schedule in Figure 10 the 'short-run aggregate supply' schedule (SRAS) to signify that it exists only in the short run. In the long run, the labour supply schedule moves to the left from $L_S(P_0)$ to $L_S(P_1)$, as workers demand compensating wage increases (see Figure 9). Eventually money wages rise by the full amount of the price increase and the economy returns to Y_0. In other words, in the long run, the economy always returns back to Y_0, and an increase in the price level from P_0 to P_1 will simply increase money wages from W_0 to W_1 (see Figure 9) without having any effect on either real output or employment. The long-run AS schedule (LRAS) is vertical at Y_0 (see Figure 10), where Y_0 is the **natural rate of output** – that is, the rate of output consistent with equilibrium in the labour market.

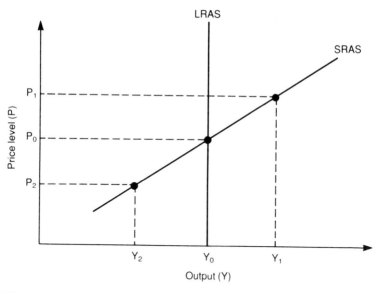

Figure 10 The natural rate of output

The economic cycle and changes in aggregate demand

We have already seen that the economy typically moves in a cyclical fashion, with output and unemployment fluctuating over time. These fluctuations can be broadly explained by reference to the behaviour of AD in the AS–AD model in Figure 11. Suppose that AD begins to increase from AD_0. In the short run, money illusion persists and the economy slides up $SRAS(P_0)$. Firms find output and profits rising, encouraging them to invest in additional capacity; households enjoy rising incomes, inducing them to borrow more and increase current consumption in the expectation of even higher incomes tomorrow. As corporate and consumer confidence rises, the increase in AD becomes self-fuelling, eventually pushing it out to AD_1. At this point, the economy has experienced a sharp increase in real output, from Y_0 to Y_1, at the cost of only a modest increase in prices (i.e. inflation) from P_0 to P_1.

Gradually, however, bottlenecks emerge on the supply side. Skill shortages develop in the labour market. And, with the demand for labour strong, as workers begin to realize that inflation is undermining the real value of their wages, unions start to bid aggressively for higher wages. As money illusion fades, the SRAS schedule drifts to the left. A destructive **wage–price spiral** is set in motion as the boom peaks, with the leftwards shift in the SRAS schedule from $SRAS(P_0)$ towards $SRAS(P_2)$ causing output to fall and prices to rise higher still. As profits and output fall, firms cut back investment plans; consumer confidence collapses; and AD shifts leftwards, from AD_1 towards AD_0. Instead of reaching a new long-run equilibrium at P_2 and Y_0, the economy instead moves into **recession**, with output falling below the natural rate Y_0, to Y_2, until prices and wages adjust sufficiently for confidence and spending to increase once more and set the cycle off again.

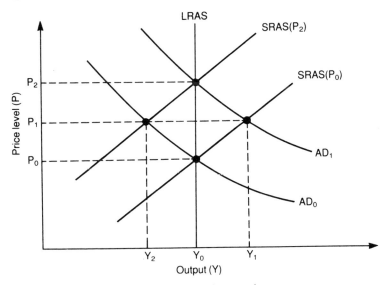

Figure 11 Changes in aggregate demand

It is clear from this account that the original increase in output from Y_0 to Y_1 is not **economic growth**; nor is the subsequent fall in output from Y_1 to Y_2 a contraction in the economy's supply side potential. Both are simply the results of the fluctuations in AD that appear to characterize free market economies. In contrast, economic growth *implies a sustained increase in the economy's capacity to produce real goods and services in the long run*, independent of changes in AD (and unemployment); that is, a rightward shift in the LRAS schedule.

Economic growth and the long-run aggregate supply schedule

Economic growth thus means a rightward shift in the LRAS – for example, from $LRAS_0$ to $LRAS_1$ in Figure 12(a). At $LRAS_1$ the economy can enjoy more goods and services at any given price level. How could such an increase in the underlying or long-run level of real output come about?

First, consider the labour market in Figure 12(c). If the labour supply were to increase – either because there was an increase in the number of workers available for employment or because the existing workforce offered more labour hours at any given money wage – this would shift the labour supply schedule to the right from L_{S0} to L_{S1}, raising equilibrium employment from L_0 to L_1. The rate of output consistent with the equilibrium in the labour market would accordingly increase from Y_0 to Y_1 for a given production function APF_0 (see Figure 12(b)), shifting the LRAS schedule from $LRAS_0$ to $LRAS_1$ in Figure 12(a).

Secondly, look at Figure 12(b). If the short-run APF were to shift upwards from APF_0 to APF_1, this would mean that, at every level of employment, a greater amount of real output can be produced than before. With equilibrium employment unchanged at L_0, the level of real output would increase, as before, from Y_0 to Y_1. The short-run APF could shift upwards if:

- the productivity of labour were to rise, because the 'quality' of labour was increased through better training and education (NB this might also increase the marginal productivity of labour, shifting the MRP – that is, the labour demand curve – to the right, but for simplicity we shall ignore this possibility in what follows);
- the capital stock were to rise, allowing each employee to produce more output for a given number of hours worked; or
- technological advances were to improve the 'quality' of the capital stock, enabling each worker to produce more output from a given amount of machinery.

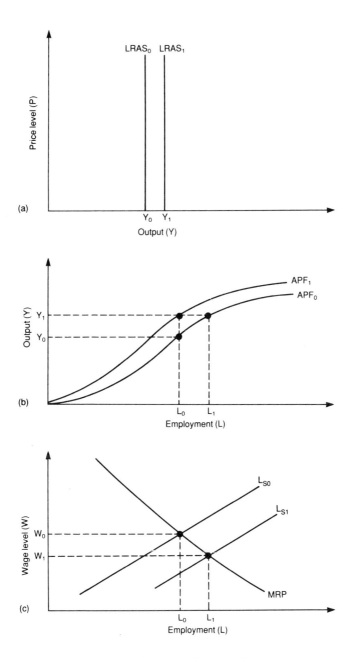

Figure 12 The sources of economic growth

To summarize, the natural rate of output will increase (i.e. the LRAS will shift to the right) if the labour supply schedule shifts to the right or if the APF function shifts upwards. There is, however, a fundamental difference between these two routes to economic growth. The gains that can be achieved from the former are necessarily finite (they are inherently **exhaustible**). While the economy can produce more output by using its existing labour force more intensively – for example, by people working longer hours, by fewer mothers staying home to look after children, by old people retiring later, etc. – we cannot achieve higher and higher output, year after year, in this way. At some point, when the entire adult population is fully employed, the rightward shift in the labour supply schedule must come to a halt. Nevertheless, in many capitalist economies, in which a very high proportion of adults are either not working (students, stay-at-home mothers, retired people, etc.), working part-time or unemployed through choice, the short-run gains in output may be substantial and continue to accrue for an extended period.

In contrast, the increases in output that can be obtained by shifts in the APF function – whether via training and education to improve the workforce, investment in plant and equipment or research and development (R&D) into new processes – can continue indefinitely over time (i.e. the increases are **sustainable**). Indeed, a moment's reflection should confirm that it is shifts in the APF function which are the source of enduring economic growth. During the last century, real output has grown at an average, year-on-year rate of 2–3 per cent. Over this time, the average number of hours worked each week has fallen steadily, while more and more young people have stayed on in school and older workers have retired earlier. Although there have been trends in the opposite direction, most notably an increase in the population and a rise in the proportion of married women working, the growth in the labour force has accounted for only a tiny proportion of the overall increase in output over the last hundred years. The primary source of the increase in our living standards has been better training and education, capital investment and R&D, rather than ever-harder work. It is to a consideration of the UK's record in each of these three areas that we now turn.

Training and education

The British system of training and education has long been regarded as a root cause of the economy's poor productivity record. Table 4 illustrates that on almost all measures of human capital acquisition, the UK compares unfavourably with the other major economies. The UK has a relatively low proportion of 16–24 year olds in further education and the least educated managerial class in Europe.

"I have heard that you do not believe there is a shortage of teachers, and that in your opinion there is, in fact, one too many in this class."

Table 4 International comparisons of human capital acquisition

	Britain	Germany	France	Japan	USA
16–24 year olds in further education (% of total)	36%	45%	n/a	54%	73%
School-leavers entering higher education (% of total)	14%	30%	35%	n/a	54%
Engineering graduates per '000 of population	14	21	15	35	n/a
Top managers with degrees (% of total)	24%	62%	65%	85%	85%

Source: Haskel and Kay (1990)

The low level of training by companies is believed to stem from the nature of the British labour market, in which workers expect to move jobs frequently – in contrast to Japan, for example, where workers often stay with the same employer throughout their working lives. This mobility reduces the incentive for firms to train their staff. Rather than expensively training workers who may then move to rival firms, it is more cost-effective for each firm to **free ride**, waiting for others to pay for training and then 'poaching' trained staff by paying marginally higher wages. The result is that, at an economy-wide level, there is a tendency for British firms collectively to undertrain staff, damaging their longer-term competitiveness. Table 5 highlights that, during the boom of the late 1980s, the percentage of firms reporting that their expansion was constrained by their inability to recruit skilled staff was many times above continental levels.

Table 5 Percentage of firms constrained by skill shortages

	Britain	Germany	France	Italy
1987	21.0	2.8	2.8	1.0
1988	26.3	3.0	3.8	2.0
1989	19.3	6.8	5.3	2.8

Source: European Commission

Governments need to start at the school gates

Economists are taking an increasing interest in the way innovation occurs and in its impact on companies. Differences among countries are harder to observe and to quantify. It is difficult even to compare the pace of successful innovation among countries, let alone to explain it. Practice in the granting of patents, the best (though inadequate) guide to the scale of innovation, varies. In Germany only one patent application in three is accepted, in Britain four out of five, in France nine out of ten.

Yet unless countries understand why some have benefited more than others from innovation, they can do little to improve their performance. Even if they do understand, change may still be difficult.

One of the boldest attempts to develop a theory that explains why the pace of innovation differs among countries is a paper written five years ago by Henry Ergas, of the OECD. He found three sets of factors:

• Those that affected the inputs into innovation, such as the quality of a country's scientific base, the presence of research institutions and, above all, its education.

• Those that influenced demand, such as receptive and sophisticated customers calling for constant innovation.

• An industrial structure that combined opportunities for intense competition with some mechanism for firms to share the financing and diffusion of scientific research.

The different ways in which these factors were combined in different countries, he argued, went a long way to explain success or failure in innovation. The role of government in shaping that combination might take one of two basic forms. In Britain, America and France, technology policy was "mission-oriented", or top-down, setting clear goals of national importance – which often meant national defence – and concentrating government R&D money on a small number of large firms. In all three countries, as the chart shows, government support for research is highly concentrated on defence, rather than on general scientific research.

The approach in Germany, Switzerland and Sweden, by contrast, was "diffusion-oriented", or bottom-up, responding more flexibly to signals from the market. Here the main goal of technology policy was to encourage innovation through the provision of a different kind of state aid: education, training and the setting of industrial standards, which help to raise quality and to spread new technologies. There was an emphasis on education, especially technical education and the training of engineers; and a high degree of specialisation in the chemical and electrical industries and in mechanical engineering.

Japan's policy was a mixture of the two main approaches. While Japanese companies were catching up with their rivals in other industrial countries, they frequently hit technical problems that they could not afford to solve individually. So the Ministry of International Trade and Industry (MITI) acted as facilitator, organising research and financing corporate participation and loans that had to be paid back if the research succeeded. The effect was to spread the risk of innovation, and also to ensure, in an economy where people rarely moved between firms, that ideas flowed from one company to another. As Japan has caught up technologically with the rest of the world, and Japanese companies have grown wealthier, they have needed MITI's help less. The main agenda for research is now set by companies themselves.

The role of government has altered also in the United States and Britain. America has found that a rising share of the commercial benefits of its defence programme has been accruing to foreign firms. In Britain, those parts of the state whose buying once shaped commercial technologies are now largely in private hands. In both countries, innovation will in future depend more on the private sector than it used to.

For a country to raise its rate of successful innovation may be extremely difficult.

As Mr Ergas puts it, "you can't become like the Germans quickly". Countries may enjoy a moment in the early years of their development when, as Japan did, they can deliberately pick the best from mature industrial cultures. For a mature culture to change itself is much harder.

The starting point is clearly education. The lack of it is a bigger reason why many poor countries are failing to catch up than is inadequate investment in physical capacity. But education needs to be diffused. A country with a scientific elite but an ill-educated workforce may be an innovator, but it will find it hard to ensure that new ideas are effectively used at home. And investment in human capital, once inadequate, is hard to bring up to scratch. Not only is it a slow process to educate under-educated adults; re-educating a workforce is labour-intensive, and draws heavily on a country's total reserve of well-trained people.

The ability of a workforce to make the best of new technologies may be a country's best competitive advantage. Wealth in raw materials, the foundation of innovation two centuries ago, barely matters: anyone can buy them. Proximity to rich markets matters less as transport costs fall, relative to the value of goods. A demanding local market is a help, but can be replaced by still more demanding foreign ones. Technologies pass rapidly from one company to another. Only that intangible, vital quality, the environment of active brains and productive skills in which companies operate, is non-transferable. To change it, governments need to start at the school gates.

Source: *The Economist*, 11 January 1992

Thinking differently:

Government R & D budget appropriations by objective, 1989

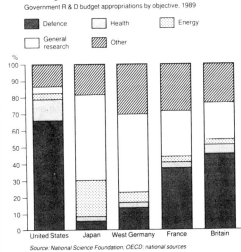

- ▨ Defence
- ▢ Health
- ▨ Energy
- ▢ General research
- ▨ Other

Source: National Science Foundation; OECD; national sources

Capital investment

Figure 13 illustrates that, expressed as a percentage of GDP, capital investment in the UK falls well below the levels enjoyed in Germany and Japan. The continuing failure of British firms to invest as heavily as their overseas rivals, despite the removal of allegedly restrictive taxes and government regulations, suggests that there may be inherent deficiencies in the way that the private sector functions. For example, critics of recent policy point to the structure of the British capital market, which – in contrast to those in Germany and Japan – allows companies that do not maximize short-term profits to be taken over against their will. As a result, British management may be deterred from undertaking the investment essential for longer-term economic success, since payback periods are typically long so that investment reduces profits in the short term. Fiscal incentives – for example, tax allowances or capital grants – may be necessary, it is argued, to induce firms to spend on R&D and invest in physical capital in such circumstances.

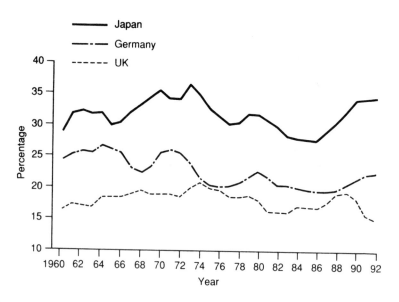

Figure 13 Gross domestic fixed capital formation as a percentage of GDP (Source: OECD)

Research and development

Tables 6 and 7 illustrate the UK's recent record on R&D. Table 6 shows that the proportion of GDP devoted to total R&D is somewhat lower than in the United States, Germany and Japan. Moreover, although this is not illustrated in Table 6, it is also the case that while all the other major trading nations increased their share of GDP devoted to R&D in the 1980s, in the UK the ratio actually declined.

Table 6 Expenditure as a percentage of GDP (1987)

	Total R&D	Government-funded R&D	
		Military	Civil
UK	2.3	0.5	0.6
Germany	2.8	0.1	1.0
France	2.3	0.5	0.9
Japan	2.9	0.0	0.4
USA	2.7	0.9	0.4

Source: OECD, Cabinet Office

Table 7 offers an international comparison of gross spending on R&D and output in terms of registered international patents (licences granted to the inventors of new products or processes to protect them from imitation). It shows that, although R&D resources appear to have been efficiently used in the UK – the average dollar cost per patent is somewhat lower for the UK than most of the other countries listed – the UK spends the least and (with the exception of France) registers the fewest patents of the five major industrial economies.

Table 7 R&D expenditure and patent registrations (1989)

	Gross R&D expenditure ($bn)	Business R&D expenditure ($bn)	Registered international patents (000s)
UK	17.0	11.3	63.4
Germany	26.7	19.5	137.1
France	19.0	11.4	56.1
Japan	58.0	40.4	115.0
USA	144.8	101.6	239.8

Source: European Commission

Conclusions

'Economists are interested in growth. The trouble is that, even by their standards, they are terribly ignorant about it. The depth of their ignorance has long been their best kept secret.'   *The Economist*

In this chapter we have seen that economic growth is a supply side phenomenon. In terms of the AS–AD model, it refers to a rightward shift in the LRAS schedule; that is, an increase in the natural rate of output. The extract reproduced from *The Economist* above might appear harsh. After all, we have seen that the basic determinants of economic growth are not in dispute. Increases in the labour supply, training and education, investment in physical capital and R&D are unambiguously the prerequisites of supply side success.

But where economists have failed to provide a clear lead is in identifying the factors that influence each of these driving forces that underpin economic growth. How does the tax and social security system affect the labour supply? Is the best way of stimulating private sector investment in human and physical capital an unregulated, laissez-faire environment? Or is activist demand management necessary to guarantee firms a healthy, growing market for their output and thereby encourage investment and risk-taking? What is the role for fiscal incentives (e.g. tax allowances, public subsidies) to promote investment and R&D? Economists have produced no clear-cut answers to these critical questions. Chapters 3 and 4 explore the basic theoretical differences between the Keynesians, who argue that government intervention is necessary for a strong supply side, and the new classical school which argues for a deregulated, liberalized economy in which the free market can operate unhindered.

KEY WORDS

Aggregate production function	Wage–price spiral
Law of diminishing returns	Recession
Marginal revenue product	Economic growth
Money illusion	Exhaustible
Real wages	Sustainable
Natural rate of output	Free ride

Reading list

Beardshaw, J., Chapter 45 in *Economics: A Student's Guide*, 3rd edn, Pitman, 1992 (note especially the data response on p. 620).

Morison, I. and Shepherdson, I., Chapter 5 in *Economics of the City*, Heinemann Educational, 1991.

Paisley, R. and Quillfeldt, J., Modules 11, 24 and 31 in *Economics Investigated*, vol 2, Collins Educational, 1992.

Turner, P., 'Investment', *Economic Review*, 1990, vol. 8 (1), pp. 28–32.

Wigley, P., 'The impact of technical innovation', *Economic Review*, 1986, vol. 4 (1), pp. 11–14.

Essay topics

1. Compare output and productivity as indicators of the economic growth of the economy. Explain in your view how, if at all, the kinds of measure required to stimulate economic growth in developing economies might differ from those required to stimulate growth in the UK. (Joint Matriculation Board, 1992)

2. What factors determine the level of investment in an economy? Why has the rate of investment generally been lower in the UK than in most other industrialized countries? (Associated Examining Board, 1989)

3. Explain what is meant by economic growth. Explain and comment on the part which capital accumulation plays in economic growth. (University of Cambridge Local Examinations Syndicate, 1991)

4. What do you understand by 'economic growth'? Outline the costs likely to be incurred in an economy undergoing rapid economic growth. To what extent can a government increase the rate of economic growth in an economy? (University of London Examinations and Assessment Council, 1991)

5. What determines the demand for labour in a given industry? Examine the factors that determine the earnings of each of the following groups of people: (i) nurses; (ii) divers working on North Sea oil rigs; (iii) law court judges. (University of London Examinations and Assessment Council, 1992)

Data Response Question 2

Growth in labour productivity in the Group of Seven industrial countries

This task is based on a question set by the Oxford & Cambridge Schools Examination Board in 1991. Study Table A, which is taken from *Economic Progress Report*, April 1989, and answer the following questions.

1. Explain what you understand by 'productivity'. The table shows international comparisons of productivity changes for the whole economy and manufacturing industry. Which set of data would you expect to be more valid and why?
2. Which country has experienced the highest overall increase in productivity since 1960? Which country has experienced the highest overall increase in productivity growth between the 1970s and 1980s?
3. Which country seems to have experienced the lowest rate of productivity increase in its *non-manufacturing* sector from 1980–88? Justify your answer.
4. State *two* factors which might influence the average annual change in labour productivity in an economy. Describe how the two factors you have identified might explain international variations shown in the table.
5. *For the UK*, comment on the likely internal and external implications of the productivity changes shown in the table.

Table A Output per person employed (average annual % changes)

	1960–70	1970–80	1980–88
Whole economy			
UK	2.4	1.3	2.5
USA	2.0	0.4	1.2
Japan	8.9	3.8	2.9
West Germany	4.4	2.8	1.8
France	4.6	2.8	2.0
Italy	6.3	2.6	2.0
Canada	2.4	1.5	1.4
Manufacturing industry			
UK	13.0	1.6	5.2
USA	3.5	3.0	4.0
Japan	8.8	5.3	3.1
West Germany	4.1	2.9	2.2
France	5.4	3.2	3.1
Italy	5.4	3.0	3.5
Canada	3.4	3.0	3.6

Chapter Three

The Keynesian approach to the supply side

'The restructuring of the UK economy must not and cannot be left to the operation of unfettered market forces. What is needed is economic planning. Planning for the market and planning of the market ... which will ensure that all aspects of recovery are properly coordinated – including training, the availability of investment finance and the deployment of technology.' Roy Hattersley, former deputy leader of the Labour party

Introduction

Until the end of the 1970s, macroeconomic policy in the UK reflected an essentially **Keynesian view** of the way the economy operated. Keynesian economists believed that, in terms of the aggregate supply and demand (AS–AD) model:

- the private sector components of aggregate demand were very unstable, so that total spending would tend to fluctuate unpredictably in the absence of government intervention; and
- the responsiveness of wages to changes in the price level – particularly in a downwards direction – was very slow.

In particular, Keynesians were concerned that, left to its own devices, aggregate demand might fall, causing the economy to operate below its natural rate of output for extended periods. With wages **sticky downwards**, rather than wages falling to clear the labour market and – by allowing firms to pass on the reduction in labour costs in the form of lower prices – pushing the economy back towards its natural rate output, the economy would instead suffer persistent unemployment. Keynesians also recognized that spontaneous increases in aggregate demand might equally well lead to inflation, as output increased above its natural rate, but they tended to regard the possibility of unemployment as the greater danger.

Keynesians accordingly recommended that governments should aim to stabilize the level of aggregate demand at the natural rate of output, neutralizing fluctuations in the private sector components of spending by appropriate adjustments in government spending, tax rates and interest rates. **Discretionary fiscal and monetary policy** of this type is normally referred to as '**fine-tuning**'. Not only was this approach to demand management urged as the only way of avoiding the twin ills of unemployment and inflation, but Keynesians also argued that stabilizing aggregate demand was the best way to promote economic growth. Because investment in research and development (R&D) and physical and human capital is so sensitive to expectations about the future level of demand for firms' finished products, Keynesians claimed that only by ensuring a high, stable level of aggregate demand would firms be able to enjoy the confidence they needed to invest for the future.

Consistent with this view of the world, which was based on the proposition that the unbridled operation of free markets would fail to propel the economy efficiently towards its natural rates of output and unemployment following changes in aggregate demand, Keynesians argued that government intervention in the supply side was also essential if countries were to maximize their growth potential. In other words, they believed that market failure was so widespread that it could only be tackled via extensive government involvement in the workings of the private sector.

Market failure and externalities

The intellectual case for market intervention is rooted in basic micro-economics and the concept of **market failure**. The market will fail to allocate resources efficiently whenever the private costs and benefits faced by producers and consumers do not completely reflect the social costs and benefits to society as a whole. For example, coal-fired power stations impose a cost on society – in the form of the environmental damage caused by acid rain – over and above the private opportunity costs (the cost of land, labour, capital, etc.) which falls upon the producer. The additional social cost is known as an **externality** or spillover effect and, being a cost, is negative. Conversely, society enjoys a wider benefit from the successful treatment of a patient with a contagious disease – insofar as the risk of other individuals being infected is reduced – over and above the private benefits which accrue to the patient concerned. The extra social benefit is a positive externality or spillover effect.

In both these examples, the presence of externalities will lead to market failure, because the free market will tend to allocate resources in a way that is socially sub-optimal. Coal-fired power stations will be operated where marginal private cost equals marginal revenue (see Figure

14), producing a profit-maximizing amount Q_0. In fact, the **social optimum** is where marginal social cost intersects marginal revenue, which would give rise to a lower quantity, Q_1, being produced. In other words, negative externalities result in socially excessive levels of production and consumption. On the other hand, the consumption of health care by those afflicted with contagious diseases will tend to be less than is socially desirable. Figure 15 shows that utility-maximizing individuals would demand an amount Q_0, which is where marginal private revenue (i.e. marginal private benefit) equals marginal cost. In fact, the socially efficient level of consumption would be Q_1, where the marginal social revenue (or benefit) schedule intersects marginal cost. Positive externalities thus lead to under-production and consumption.

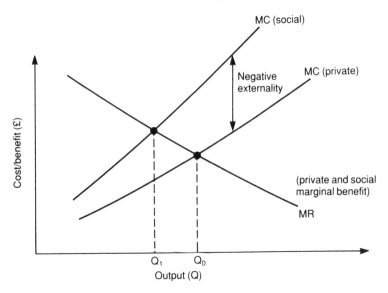

Figure 14 Negative externalities

How do considerations of externalities relate to the supply side? Keynesians argue that many of the key determinants of economic growth are plagued by positive externalities, so that the free market will tend to under-invest in R&D and physical and human capital. As a result, the growth rate will be slower than socially optimal. Consider basic R&D. Expenditure on pioneering R&D to develop new products and processes is expensive and innovating firms are only imperfectly protected from imitators by patent laws (which prohibit rivals 'cloning' the innovators' new products). Patent law is often difficult to enforce

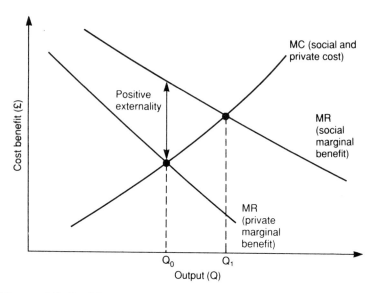

Figure 15 Positive externalities

and followers have a significant cost advantage over the innovator, since they do not have to recoup the initial R&D costs. When Sony first launched the 'Walkman' cassette-player, for example, it temporarily enjoyed a monopoly position and prices in real terms were 400–500 per cent higher than they are today. Within months of the product reaching the market, however, it was followed by a host of cheaper cassette-players from rival manufacturers, which quickly drove down the market price. Sony's R&D thus had a positive spillover effect from the point of view of other firms. Since Sony could not prevent the technology it had invented from becoming public knowledge, the other firms profited from Sony's R&D without having to pay for it; in other words, the benefit to society as a whole far exceeded the private benefits to Sony.

Given the presence of positive externalities, Keynesians argued, the amount of R&D undertaken by firms in aggregate is likely to be **socially sub-optimal,** with many firms preferring to wait for their rivals to make the technological breakthroughs. It is significant that, in Japan, where the corporate system of *keiretzu* ties together otherwise independent companies through a complex series of interlocking directorships and shareholdings, companies do not have the same incentive to free-ride on the R&D of others and Japan is a clearly established world leader in high-tech industries. In the UK, on the other hand,

Keynesians concluded that the same effect could only be achieved through government intervention.

Training and education may also be subject to similar effects. Imagine that in the absence of publicly provided training and education, a private company decides to offer training services to subscribing firms. While each firm would be paying to send its staff on the training courses, each guesses (rightly) that, by not paying, the benefits can be enjoyed by 'free-riding' at their neighbours' expense, since they may be able to poach trained workers from their rivals by paying only slightly above the present market wage. As a result, many firms refuse to subscribe and the ensuing service is socially sub-optimal. An alternative solution would be to provide the training publicly, financing it with a tax which each company will willingly pay, in the knowledge that the scheme constrains their neighbours to join with them in a collectively advantageous enterprise.

Information and economic coordination

Just as Keynesians were sceptical about the ability of free markets to keep the economy at its natural rates of output and unemployment over time, so they believed that the 'invisible hand' was ill-suited to the task of coordinating investment across a modern economy. For the car industry, for example, to invest in new, high-tech plant and equipment, its managers had to be confident of the future demand for their products – a guarantee provided by the government's commitment to maintain a high level of aggregate demand. But if the industry's expansion was not to be choked off by shortages of machinery and skilled workers, it required that the capital goods industry, in turn, was geared up to provide the extra machine tools needed by car producers; and that the school system was equipping school leavers with the knowledge to use the new machinery. How was this degree of coordination to be achieved across a complex, interdependent economy, Keynesians asked?

Given the long lead times between the decision to produce and the delivery of the finished product, Keynesians doubted that price signals alone would work to coordinate the plans of different sectors. How were machine tool makers to know that the car industry intended a major expansion? When the increase in investment started to take place, the car industry would accordingly find the machine tool sector without the capacity to respond. While shortages would drive up the price of machine tools, thereby stimulating an increase in output, it might take months, even years, before supply fully responded to the increased demand from the car industry. Similarly, it might take years for local schools to adjust the mix of their vocational training courses to meet the changing needs of the car industry.

Can Keynes offer a route for the nineties?

Peter Clarke

The eighties were not kind to Keynes's memory, still less to the credibility of his doctrines. The rise of Thatcherism in Britain and of Reaganomics in the United States brought explicit rejection of a Keynesian approach to economic problems – denounced as "the policies that failed before". That man Keynes, Ronald Reagan said, didn't even have a degree in economics.

This fact only seems remarkable in our own day, when economics is often regarded as abstruse and jargon-ridden. For young Maynard was hardly educationally deprived. Born in 1883, he came from an academic family and had been sent to Eton before going to Cambridge to read mathematics at King's College. Only then did he turn to economics, and his total formal tuition amounted to eight hours, given by a family friend. But the friend was Alfred Marshall, the leading British economist of the day, who passed on to his gifted pupil the lifelong conviction that economics was "a moral science".

It was a useful way of thinking about the means by which markets worked. These means, however, were not economic laws, demanding blind obedience: they were simply means to an end. The real point was to ally value judgements about what was desirable with technical expertise about what was feasible. It was the *combination* of gifts required – as mathematician, historian, statesman and philosopher – which excited Keynes about becoming an economist. "An easy subject, at which very few excel!"

Ultimately, Keynes used Marshall's method to challenge the economic orthodoxy on which he had been brought up. What orthodox theory said was that in the long run market forces would find their own equilibrium. What was implied, was that this equilibrium would offer full employment of all resources, notably of labour.

On a theoretical level, the problem of people who were willing to work, but unable to find jobs, did not arise. Of course, in the real world economists could see that unemployment existed from time to time, because of all sorts of reasons workers were pricing themselves out of jobs: they were in the wrong industries, or in trade unions which had wrongly assessed what the market could bear. These were problems for the market to solve; the Treasury's job was simply to balance the Budget.

Keynes challenged the notion that the economy is self-righting. This was the basis of his own claim to "revoluntionise the way the world thinks about economic problems".

It was not until the Thirties that Keynes focused his energies on economic theory itself. Within a surprisingly short time, he was arguing out his new theory of effective demand. Instead of investment depending upon prior saving – the orthodox story – savings were generated by an initial act of investment. It was investment that generated higher incomes, which in turn led to greater savings. Equilibrium between savings and investment would be achieved but, contradicting orthodox theory, Keynes said this could happen while output was still below full capacity or full employment. It might mean that the economy was stuck in a position of high unemployment.

The *General Theory* thus gave a wholly new account of how the economy worked – or failed to work. No longer did Keynes point to particular obstructions in the real world as the crucial reason prices were prevented from making the sort of adjustments which would clear the market. He argued now that reductions in wages or interest rates, even if forthcoming, might be simply incapable of restoring full employment. In such circumstances, only government could break the deadlock.

The *General Theory*, for all its revolutionary thinking, was largely silent on policy. Keynes, moreover, was fairly tentative and cautious in his subsequent practical recommendations, well aware that there were bottlenecks in production and reluctant to advance a practicable target for "full employment" above a level of 95 per cent. By 1937, indeed, with symptoms of recovery at last apparent in Britain, he ceased to advise further expansion of demand. But if he now urged caution over

Budgetary policy, this was because his theory was symmetrical, not one-sided. "Just as it was advisable for the government to incur debt during the slump, so for the same reasons it is now advisable they should incline to the opposite policy."

The point was that no "invisible hand" is at work to guide the course of investment. Keynes therefore accepted the necessity for some kind of planning if unemployment were to be controlled. It was essential for government to act as a make-weight in an economy which lacked self-righting properties. Hence the continued relevance of his ideas about using the Budget to promote economic recovery rather than placing all our trust in market forces – a trust which may be misplaced.

And today? Keynes would have been the first to say that it is no use poring over policy suggestions which are now more than 50 years old for detailed guidance on the problems of the nineties. His own message was clear: "We have to invent new wisdom for a new age."

Source: *Independent on Sunday*, 29 March 1992

In the meantime, the intended expansion of the car industry, while having set in motion increases in the capacity of its suppliers, would have been initially held back by the shortage of machine tools and skilled labour. Disadvantaged in this way, the car industry might find itself losing ground to overseas competitors, forcing it to reassess its plans for expansion. By the time the extra machine tools and skilled labour became available, the domestic car industry might be so weakened that it could no longer carry out its original plans. In other words, when there are long time lags between firms receiving price signals and actually responding with changes in production, events may have moved on so that by the time the supply side responses actually come, they are no longer appropriate.

Keynesians concluded that the invisible hand was therefore likely to be incapable of coordinating investment decisions across the economy in a way that would maximize the rate of economic growth. While the guarantee of high and stable levels of aggregate demand would undoubtedly help, Keynesians argued that governments should play a more explicit role in ensuring balanced growth. This attitude to the functioning of the economy became influential in the early 1960s, following the apparent success of national economic planning in countries as diverse as the former Soviet Union, Japan and France.

The Keynesian supply side prescription

As we have seen, Keynesians were highly sceptical of the ability of free markets to function efficiently. They argued that the widespread existence of externalities and market failure and the inability of the price mechanism to carry the information necessary to coordinate economic decision-making would result in sub-optimal rates of economic growth. Persuaded by the Keynesians' diagnosis of Britain's economic ills, successive governments during the period 1945–79 concentrated their supply side efforts on three main fronts:

- attempts to plan the economy;
- taking firms into public ownership;
- government-directed investment and industrial restructuring.

Conclusions

From 1945 until 1979, macroeconomic policy in the UK followed the policy prescriptions of the Keynesian tradition. In principle, demand management was used to stabilize aggregate demand at a level consistent with the natural rate of output, although in practice political pressures often resulted in governments overstimulating demand, reaping the electoral benefits of a temporary lower rate of unemployment at the cost of higher inflation in the longer term. While an important justification of fine-tuning was that it promoted economic growth by providing the conditions in which firms could invest with confidence, Keynesians also prescribed a raft of explicit supply side policies. These were justified on the grounds of widespread market failure and included indicative planning, nationalization and various measures, both indirect (e.g. fiscal carrots and sticks) and direct, to stimulate R&D and investment in physical and human capital.

These policies were not without their critics. New classical economists attacked fine-tuning as inflationary and counterproductive, rejecting the notion that the private sector was inherently unstable and claiming that wages adjusted rapidly to changes in prices. More significantly, they also dismissed the proposition that the price mechanism was unable to coordinate economic activity and generate the optimal levels of investment, claiming instead that the UK's supply side weaknesses resulted from excessive government interference in the economy, rather than any inherent deficiency in the private sector. They alleged that the growth of the public sector, which took output and employment decisions on non-commercial grounds, and the increase in taxes necessary to finance the welfare state, had seriously damaged the incentives to invest. It is to this critique of the Keynesian era and the policy recommendations of the new classical school that we turn in Chapter 4.

KEY WORDS

Keynesian view	Market failure
Sticky downwards	Externality
Discretionary fiscal and	Social optimum
monetary policy	Socially sub-optimal
Fine-tuning	

Reading list

Gardner, N., *Decade of Discontent: The Changing British Economy Since 1973*, Basil Blackwell, 1987, pp. 1–66.

Hattersley, R. and Jones, D., Chapters 7, 8, 10, 13 and 14 in *Economic Priorities for a Labour Government*, Macmillan, 1987.

Healey, N. and Parker, D., Chapter 8 in *Current Topics in Applied Economics*, Anforme, 1988.

Wilkinson, M., Chapters 4 and 5 in *Equity and Efficiency*, Heinemann Educational, 1993.

Essay topics

1. Discuss the economic relationships between consumption, income and investment. (Associated Examining Board, 1990)
2. Analyse the likely impact of a significant cut in the standard rate of income tax on: (a) the level of employment; (b) the rate of inflation; (c) the balance of payments. (University of London Examinations and Assessment Council, 1991)
3. Explain what you understand by aggregate demand. Comment upon the use and limitations of demand management as a means of achieving macroeconomic policy objectives in the UK economy. (University of Cambridge Local Examinations Syndicate, 1991)
4. How does fiscal policy affect the level of national income? (Oxford & Cambridge Schools Examination Board, 1991)

Data Response Question 3

The PSBR and consumer spending

This task is based on a question set by the University of Oxford Delegacy of Local Examinations in 1991. Read the passage, which is adapted from an article entitled 'Is the "Thatcher Experiment" still on course?' by David Vines (*Royal Bank of Scotland Review*, 1989), and answer the following questions.

1. Explain what is meant by the 'PSBR'.
2. In your own words, explain and comment upon what, according to Vines, was regarded as a 'prudent' fiscal policy in the early eighties.
3. Explain how the behaviour of the private sector in the late 1980s differed from that of the late 1970s.
4. What would you expect to be the economic consequences of this change in behaviour, and why would they be 'worrying'?
5. In the light of the changed behaviour discussed in (3) and (4), how would Keynesian economists expect a prudent fiscal policy to change?

We have reached an important position as regards fiscal policy. This is also very different from what was believed in the early eighties. It was then thought that a prudent fiscal policy which involved reducing the PSBR to a small percentage of GDP, or perhaps zero, would avoid 'crowing out' of private sector investment and leave sufficient resources in the economy to be devoted to the accumulation of wealth.

We were asked to believe that monetary policy would ensure that there would be no inflationary excess of demand over output and that a prudent fiscal policy would ensure that this demand was properly distributed between consumption and investment. The PSBR is now forecast to be about minus £14.2 billion which is about minus 3 per cent of GDP and roughly similar to last year; but last year many observers were saying that this fiscal policy was too lax! Why such a change?

The reason for this is the behaviour of private sector spending. Keynesian economists (who ran for cover in the early 1980s) have always known that there is no such thing as a 'prudent fiscal policy' in the abstract; fiscal policy can only be said to be prudent in the light of the private sector's decisions. And, in the United Kingdom recently, these have been historically abnormal.

The fundamental reason is the behaviour of consumer spending. The personal sector savings ratio, now 5 per cent, was as low as 3 per cent in mid-1988. This compares with 10–15 per cent in the late 1970s . . . this personal sector savings ratio is not only abnormally below the levels witnessed through much of the last two decades but it is also worrying: at present the British private sector does not want to save to make resources available for investment. This is why the government needs to run a large surplus.

Chapter Four
New classical theories of the supply side

'We need a complete change of attitude towards the way our economy works . . . to remove the constraints imposed by the tax system and by the unduly large role previously played by the government, releasing initiative and enterprise.' HM Treasury, 1979

Introduction

In the late 1970s, the policy prescriptions of the Keynesians came under increasing attack from a group of economists known as the 'new classical school'. Initially, these critics of the prevailing orthodoxy attracted most attention for their claim that excessive monetary growth was the root of the inflation then plaguing the British economy. This insistence that money, which played only a minor role in Keynesian explanations of inflation, was the key factor determining prices quickly acquired these mavericks the label 'monetarists'. *But their differences with the Keynesians were much more fundamental than the question of whether monetary, as opposed to fiscal, policy was the more powerful influence on aggregate demand.* Their theories amounted to a revival, albeit with modifications and refinements, of the classical school of macroeconomics that had been ousted by the Keynesian 'revolution' in the 1930s. As their ideas became more widely known, not least as a result of the enthusiasm with which they were taken up by Mrs Thatcher's Conservative government after 1979, the more accurate designation of the 'new classical' school gradually gained acceptance.

The new classical economist believed that the private sector was inherently efficient, with unfettered labour and goods markets clearing quickly and the economy automatically tending to its natural rate of output. They concluded, moreover, that far from being necessary to stabilize aggregate demand and thereby promote investment and economic growth, discretionary demand management policy had in fact been positively destabilizing. This was because, when aggregate demand changed spontaneously, the private sector rapidly began to adapt its price and wage-fixing behaviour. Policy adjustments by the government, which inevitably took time to implement, simply had the effect of pushing the economy further in the direction it was already moving, causing it to overshoot the natural rate of output and resulting in either inflation or unemployment. For example, if aggregate demand were to fall in Figure 16 from AD_0 to AD_1, the short-run aggregate supply schedule would quickly shift down from $SRAS(P_0)$ to $SRAS(P_2)$, as lower prices fed through into lower wage settlements. If the government responded to the initial contraction in demand by relaxing fiscal and monetary policy, driving aggregate demand back to AD_0, as these lagged effects spread through the economy the economy would slide up its new short-run aggregate supply schedule, $SRAS(P_2)$, throwing the economy back into disequilibrium just as it was recovering from the initial demand side 'shock'.

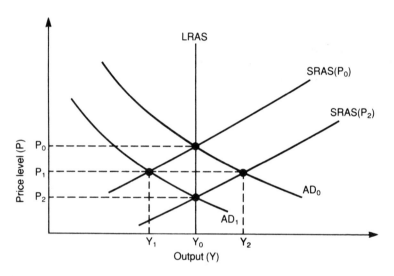

Figure 16 Destabilizing demand management

Moreover, to the extent that markets did not appear to clear as smoothly as new classical economists claimed, they argued that any sluggishness was due to the interference of government, which had injected damaging distortions into the economic system. Nationalization, state controls and regulations, and high taxes were singled out for particular criticism in this regard. In contrast to the Keynesians, who had highlighted the importance of market failure as the primary source of supply side weakness in the British economy, the new classical economists stressed the need to liberate and properly reward individual **enterprise**.

The rationale of new classical supply side policies

Like Keynesians, the new classical school faced the task of explaining why it is that some countries undertake more research and development (R&D) and invest more in physical and human capital than others, thereby reaping the benefits of faster economic growth. In providing their answer to this conundrum, the new classical school emphasized the importance of individual economic agents, motivated by self-interest and reacting to the incentives and sanctions provided by the economic system within which they operate. In this, the new classical economists drew upon a long tradition, extending back to Adam Smith's famous book *Wealth of Nations*, and revitalized by the more recent ideas of Hayek and the so-called '**Austrian school**' (see the boxed extract). The latter stressed the vital function of competitive markets in providing people with the incentives to seek out information about profitable opportunities for production and exchange. Information concerning the most efficient methods of production and which goods are most valued by consumers will only be discovered by economic agents with a personal incentive to do so, because they expect to benefit as a consequence.

The key economic agents on the supply side of the economy are the various categories of producers – **entrepreneurs,** managers and workers – together with investors (those people who are postponing consumption by investing in productive assets) and their advisers, the financial institutions. According to the new classical view, entrepreneurs are motivated by the expectation of profit to discover and supply products that consumers want and to use efficient production methods. The stimulus to serve consumers is best provided in competitive markets. If there are few rival suppliers to whom consumers can turn when they are dissatisfied, then firms can still earn profits even while operating with costs above the feasible minimum or failing to produce the type and quality of goods consumers prefer. Without the stimulus of competition, a firm has less inducement to organize its workforce efficiently, to provide its employees with incentives to work efficiently and to satisfy customers' wants.

The new classical economists' scepticism about the ability of governments to improve economic performance by means of direct intervention is based on the argument that governments cannot obtain the requisite information about the most efficient ways of allocating resources. The market is more efficient at discovering and transmitting such information because it relies on specialists in particular market niches obtaining and using information about the kinds of goods and services demanded by consumers and about the cheapest methods of production. The economy is in a constant state of flux as changes occur in technical knowledge, in the prices of raw materials or in consumer tastes.

In praise of Hayek

The century's greatest champion of economic liberalism died on 24 March, at the age of 92

Like Maynard Keynes, Friedrich von Hayek achieved fame less for what he wrote than for what others said he wrote. The economic philosophy he developed over six decades, and especially during the 20 years he spent at the London School of Economics after 1931, was not, as so many now suppose, "neo-conservatism". Still less was it the underlying rationale for Thatcherism or Reaganomics, whatever those might be. And as it happens, the supposed "godfather of monetarism" had no time whatever for the assumptions on which that narrow, technocratic doctrine is based. None of these labels fits the great man. Call him instead an original thinker in the tradition of classical liberalism – perhaps the century's finest.

Much of Hayek's work is difficult; all of it is idiosyncratic. His writings seem especially peculiar to economists trained in the modern Anglo-American way, because Hayek rejected that school's paradigm: the idea of a static system in which certain stable properties (many buyers, many sellers, perfect information, homogeneous goods) yield certain stable results (an optimal allocation of resources). Hayek was interested in markets and economies as systems in flux. In his scheme, sequences of events, not states of affairs, were the object of study. Anglo-American economics starts by abstracting from change and time – and is then obliged to reintroduce them, with difficulty, to make its analysis more informative. Hayek, and others of the so-called Austrian school, put change and time at the centre from the outset.

Other themes seem to follow naturally from that perspective. They recur in almost everything Hayek wrote.

The most crucial is the notion of a market as a process of discovery. Modern economies are vastly complicated. Somehow they must process immense quantities of information – concerning the tastes and incomes of consumers, the outputs and costs of producers, future products and methods of production, and the myriad interdependences of all of the above. The task of gathering this information, let alone making sense of it, is beyond any designing intelligence. But it is not beyond the market, which yields "spontaneous order" out of chaos. Hayek looked on the miracle of the invisible hand with the same delight as Adam Smith. He celebrated it anew, and made it his mission to understand it....

Co-operation makes impossible demands on the ability of large groups to gather and process information; competition is the only way to regulate interaction on this scale. The attempt to extend co-operation beyond its natural limits is not just doomed to fail, it is also extremely dangerous. Competition requires no designer; co-operation on the large scale does. Socialism, the most ambitious and misguided form of large-scale co-operation, cannot be implemented without a strong central authority. Hence another Hayekian theme: economic and political freedom are tied together.

Hayek carried his distrust of the state to an implausible extreme. He argued, in effect, that governments could never legitimately pursue goals of their own – not even on behalf of "society" (a term he disliked). Goals and values are for individuals themselves to choose. The state ought not to be a policy-maker with an agenda, but an arrangement of rules that allow people to go about their business in peace. Hayek was especially worried about the appearance of legitimacy that majoritarian democracy lends to the interventionist state. Where, he asked, is the minority's defence against the power of the majority? On Hayek's view, most of the economic powers that modern governments take for granted – from industrial policy to redistribution of income – are not merely ill-advised but immoral.

Few could find that position satisfactory. The modern state may presume too much – but to deal with some economic ills, collective action (and hence the coercion that Hayek detested) is almost universally agreed upon. In some cases, moreover, it is simply inescapable. Hayek's greatest weakness was that he had almost nothing to say about market-failure. This justification for state action is often falsely invoked – but sometimes the argument is convincing. In cleaning up the environment, for instance, the state must indeed intervene on behalf of society: externalities mean that free markets are unable to discover the outcomes that individuals seek.

Source: *The Economist*, 28 March 1992

Competition at work!

It is also dynamic, in the sense that it continually generates new applications for technical knowledge and adapts rapidly and smoothly to changes in the forces of demand and supply, if and only if individual economic agents have the appropriate incentives.

On this view of the world, the role of government is to ensure that the laws, regulations and institutions operate so as to provide economic agents with the required incentives and information. Direct intervention by government – with the objective of determining which goods should be produced, where investment should be directed, which areas of research should be investigated or what prices should be charged – is doomed to be inefficient. Governments cannot obtain the requisite information at the right time and are pressured by special interest (or 'rent-seeking') groups to allocate resources to satisfy their own specific interests.

The rationale of new classical supply side policies is thus derived directly from this view of how markets operate in allocating resources, in contrast to the comparative inefficiency of government regulation. The general aim of new classical supply side policies is to strengthen and extent competitive market forces and to alter existing laws and regulations in order to improve the incentives for individuals to seek out productive activities. Inspired by the new classical school, the Conservative government that came to power in 1979 rejected the Keynesian supply side policies that it inherited and introduced a raft of new measures which included:

- **privatization** of public enterprises;
- **deregulation** of the goods and capital markets;
- reform of the tax and social security system to increase incentives to work and invest; and
- legislative changes designed to liberalize the labour market.

The last two dimensions of the Conservative government's supply side programme are discussed more fully in Chapters 5 and 6, but at this point it is useful to review the key features of recent supply side policy.

Privatization

Privatization – that is the narrow sense of **denationalization** (selling state-owned assets to the private sector) – best promotes competition if the transfer of ownership is accompanied by deregulation or the breaking up of a state monopoly into several competing businesses. The best example of such a privatization is that of the National Bus Company, which was gradually sold off during 1986–87 as separate companies, many of them to the existing management groups. However, the bulk of the large-scale privatizations – e.g. British Telecom, British Gas, British Airways and the British Airports Authority – have involved the transfer intact of a state monopoly or dominant firm to the private sector. This pattern has been much criticized by new classical economists on the grounds that it does little to promote competition and efficiency.

Some privatizations have been accompanied by **deregulation** and it is often argued that is the latter, rather than the former, that actually promotes competition. For instance, the privatization of British Telecom (BT) in 1985 was preceded by the 1981 Telecommunications Act, which permitted certain kinds of private equipment to be connected to the BT network and allowed a newly formed private consortium, Mercury, to compete for domestic business. Mercury now uses optical fibre cables for business communications which it connects with the BT network. As a result of the 1981 Act new products, such as car telephones and more sophisticated receivers, have mushroomed.

The experience of privatization is fully discussed in a companion book, *Privatization and the Public Sector*, by Bryan Hurl.

Deregulation of goods and capital markets

A regulated market is one in which laws, and the related regulations that authorized bodies make, limit the actions of producers and consumers. These regulations are often justified as being needed to protect customers and workers from the consequences of their inadequate information about the quality of goods or hazards of working conditions. All markets are regulated by health and safety laws and consumer protection legislation, but many have or have had specific regulations which limit competition and act in the interests of established suppliers.

Deregulation involves reducing the number of regulations by removing those that serve only to restrict competition and do little to enhance the safety of customers or workers. The objectives of deregulation are to increase competition between existing suppliers and between them and new suppliers who can now enter the market. This should reduce costs and stimulate the provision of new services for which there is a demand. Recent examples of deregulation in the UK are buses and the Stock Exchange.

The 1980 Transport Act deregulated long-distance coach travel. Restrictions on operators entering the market were removed and limited to safety standards. Many small companies entered the market which was dominated by the then state-owned National Bus Company, which fought back successfully by cutting fares and introducing new routes. There has been a significant fall in long-distance coach fares and a consequent rise in the number of passenger-miles travelled. In 1986, local bus services were deregulated. Until then private operators had been unable to enter the market without securing a local authority licence for the route. Under the new legislation local authorities are required to invite tenders for their local bus routes and award the tender to the cheapest contractor. Subsidies to bus services have also been cut. The objective of the legislation is to reduce the costs of bus travel and to provide those services for which there is a local demand by allowing the entry of small operators.

The Stock Exchange historically operated practices which limited competition. It had a system of fixed commissions for buying and selling shares, so that all firms charged the same agreed price. Another restriction was that single capacity jobbers (firms holding shares and bonds in order to make a market in them) had to be separate from stockbrokers (firms who bought and sold securities on behalf of investors); single capacity therefore limited the entry of financial institutions into the Stock Exchange. When the Office of Fair Trading threatened legal action against fixed commissions, the Stock Exchange agreed to abandon the practice of charging fixed commissions voluntarily, in return for exemption from prosecution for restrictive practices. The much publicized 'Big Bang' of October 1986 marked the day on which the Stock Exchange introduced computerized trading, dual capacity and variable commissions. These changes ushered in considerable restructuring of City financial institutions, the entry of many foreign firms and a considerable growth in financial activity. Other areas which have been deregulated include opticians and house conveyancing.

Deregulation and '1992'

The final decade of the twentieth century promises to witness a further bonfire of regulatory obstacles to free competition on an altogether wider scale. The European Community's so-called '1992' programme to 'complete the single market' attempts to create a genuinely free market in goods, services, labour and capital. The ED has either harmonized or abolished a wide range of official restrictions and regulations that act as 'non-tariff barriers', protecting small, inefficient national producers from outside competition. Table 8 sets out the package of EC legislative changes.

The fundamental problem was that centuries of separate political development by the 12 member states spawned a dozen mutually inconsistent sets of legislation regarding technical and health and safety standards, segmenting the EC into small, discrete markets served by small-scale producers. For instance, the EC has 50 tractor manufacturers competing for annual sales of 200 000 units; in the United States, a market of similar size is served by only four large producers. In the EC, it has been almost impossible to manufacture a tractor that will sell in more than two or three countries without significant engineering alterations. Figure 17 shows that this pattern is replicated across other industrial sectors (e.g. white goods, soft drinks, alcoholic beverages). Inconsistent national standards fragment the market and perpetuate inefficient small-scale production.

Table 8 The 1992 package of EC measures

Non-tariff barriers at which proposals are aimed	Number of proposals
Technical barriers and harmonization	78
Veterinary and plant hygiene	83
Financial services and capital market controls	26
Free movement of persons	21
Control of goods	10
Transport	11
Indirect taxation	22
Public procurement	6
Telecommunications	5
Intellectual property	8
Company law	12
Total	282

Source: European Commission

There is nothing like 'corpses on the lawn' for discouraging new entrants

Sir Gordon Borrie

When the bus industry was deregulated, it was brought fully within the scope of the general competition legislation and it was not thought necessary to create an Ofbus. Competition was being encouraged from the outset, primarily by privatisation and the breaking up of the NBC*, and it was thought there was no need for special regulation. Predictably, the structure proved to be unstable, and there have been many subsequent mergers resulting in some quite large, if geographically spread, new-style operators. Several mergers have been referred on my advice to the MMC and divestment ordered following adverse reports from the MMC, but challenge in the courts has made the future of this application of competition policy uncertain. Further, the established local operators have exploited the many advantages they have over potential, usually small scale, entrants, which advantages reduce in practice the *contestability* of the bus market. One advantage is control of an essential facility, such as a bus station. It is an anomaly, perhaps, that whereas the 1985 Act requires that the operator of a publicly-owned bus station shall make that facility available to all operators on a non-discriminatory basis, there is so such provision for privately-owned bus stations. In 1986, acting under the Competition Act 1980, I did rule as anti-competitive the refusal by

*State-owned National Bus Company

Southern Vectis, the dominant bus operator on the Isle of Wight, to allow a small competitor to use its bus station at Newport because of the lack of any alternative, reasonably comparable, facility. I accepted an undertaking from Southern Vectis to allow competitors access on payment of a non-discriminatory cost-related fee.

Another feature of the bus market since deregulation, which may also be of wider relevance, is *strategic predatory behaviour* – usually the use of predatory prices – designed to eliminate competitors and deter subsequent new entrants. In one writer's phrase: there is nothing like some 'corpses on the lawn' for discouraging new entry. Up to the end of 1990 we have had 105 complaints of predatory behaviour by established bus operators against (usually small) new entrants.

The dividing line between predatory and aggressive, but wholly legitimate, competitive behaviour is a notoriously difficult one to define and apply and, generally, I believe that competition authorities (and regulators) should err on the side of caution before taking action in response to allegations of predation. But where the market structure and characteristics of the firms involved suggest that predation could well be a profitable strategy in the long-run sense, then intervention may well be justified.

Sir Gordon Borrie is Director General of the Office of Fair Trading.

Source: *Economic Affairs*, Sept. 1991

Table 9 shows that the prices of 'tradeable' goods and services still vary widely across EC countries; in an integrated market, differences should reflect only transport costs when expressed in a common currency, reflecting the **law of one price**. Once the 1992 measures have been fully implemented, competition within the EC is likely to intensify dramatically, driving prices down and strengthening the supply side of the Community as a whole.

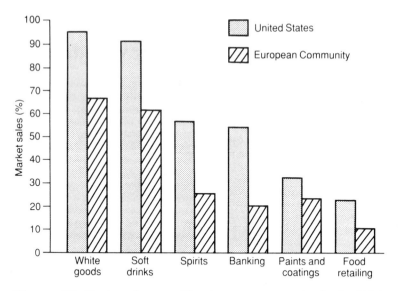

Figure 17 Market shares of five largest companies in the USA and the EC

Tax and social security

Whether a tax is levied according to a person's ability to pay or according to his or her expenditure, it reduces the rate of return that an individual obtains from market activities – like working for a wage or investing in shares or other assets with taxable yields. The new classical argument is that, as a consequence of taxation, people will be less willing to engage in market activities, as well as shifting into market activities that are less heavily taxed. They will also risk not reporting all their income to the tax authorities; in other words, they will work in the 'black' or 'shadow' economy.

Table 9 Prices in the EC (common currency, Belgian price = 100)

Country	German cars	Pharmaceuticals	Life insurance	Domestic appliances
Belgium	100	100	100	100
France	115	78	75	130
Germany	127	174	59	117
Italy	129	80	102	110
Netherlands	n/a	164	51	105
UK	142	114	39	93

Source: *European Economy*

The more extreme new classical economists have maintained that the proportion of national income taken in tax is too high and that reducing this proportion would stimulate economic growth (see also Chapter 5). There is little empirical evidence to support this contention at such a high level of aggregation or for levels of taxation that have actually been experienced. As Figure 18 shows, there has in the past been little relationship between the proportion of a country's national income that is taxed and its growth rate.

Concern about the inefficiency caused by the structure of the tax sys-

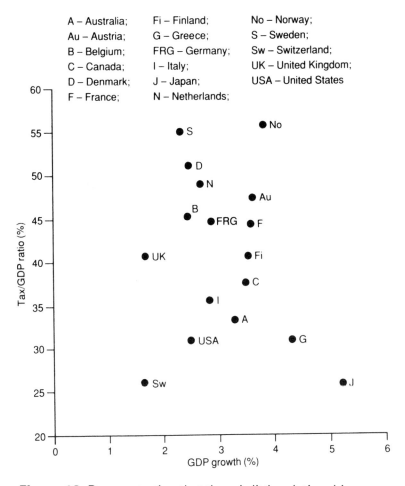

Figure 18 Demonstration that there is little relationship between tax rate and growth in GDP

tem, rather than the level of taxes, is far more widespread and stimulated tax reforms in the 1980s in a number of countries. The tax structure refers to the different kinds of activities that are taxed and the differential tax rates applied – for example, what kind of income is taxed and what rates of tax different income earners have to pay.

Taxes also distort choices. If a good is taxed more heavily than others, consumers will buy less of it and switch to other goods. This reduces consumers' utility because they would prefer, in the absence of the tax, to buy more of the good. This consideration is particularly pertinent for the taxation of income from investment, since the tax structure has resulted in huge differences in the post-tax rate of return from investing in different kinds of assets. Mortgage-interest tax relief increases the private rate of return from investing in a house compared with investing in a business. Tax relief on premiums for life assurance and pension contributions has meant that individuals get a better return from saving via life assurance and pension fund schemes than by investing directly in shares.

New classical economists also argue that social security benefits discourage work by low income earners. The higher the benefits received when unemployed relative to income from working, the less incentive there is for people to seek work. This is a controversial argument because it can imply policies to cut the incomes of those who are already poor. Recent policy with regard to tax and social security is examined further in Chapter 5.

The labour market

Labour market reform was at the forefront of the Conservative government's supply side strategy during the 1980s. Ministers variously accused trade unions of inhibiting economic progress and blunting the UK's overseas competitiveness by the use of restrictive work practices and overmanning, and preventing the flexible operation of the labour market by holding wages above their market-clearing levels and thereby causing higher unemployment.

The Conservative government's attempts to reform the labour market have proved electorally popular. By the late 1970s, there was a growing public conviction that the trade unions had become too powerful. This view was reinforced during the so-called 'winter of discontent' of 1978–79, when there was major disputes in the health service and the road haulage industry as unions challenged the Labour government's pay guidelines. Unions were also widely perceived as refusing to abandon restrictive practices, thereby hindering technological change and depressing the growth of labour productivity.

Since 1979, a series of statutes has placed restrictions on trade union activity. The objectives and effects of these reforms is considered in more detail in Chapter 6.

Conclusions

This chapter has examined the new classical approach to the supply side. We have seen that, in contrast to the Keynesian school of thought, new classical economists believe that free markets, left to their own devices, will best allocate resources between competing ends in an efficient way. They are sceptical of the Keynesian's insistence on government intervention to strengthen the supply side. Indeed, new classical economists typically regard attempts by the state to control private sector activity as counter-productive, blaming the UK's relatively poor postwar supply side record on excessive government interference. Inspired by this theoretical approach to the supply side, the post-1979 Conservative governments have directed policy at 'freeing the market', by privatizing nationalized industries, rationalizing the tax and social security system, and reforming the UK's notoriously inflexible labour market. Chapters 5 and 6 now consider the operation and performance of recent supply side policy in each of these areas.

KEY WORDS

Enterprise	Deregulation
Austrian School	Denationalization
Entrepreneur	Law of one price
Privatization	Shadow economy

Reading list

Cook, M., and Healey, N., Chapter 4 in *Current Topics in International Economics*, Anforme, 1990.

Healey, N., and Parker, D., Chapter 7 in *Current Topics in Economic Theory*, Anforme, 1990.

Hurl, B., *Privatization and the Public Sector*, 2nd edn, Heinemann Educational, 1992.

National Institute of Economic and Social Research, Chapter 4 in *The UK Economy*, 2nd edn, Heinemann Educational, 1992

Smith, D., Chapters 1, 6 and 7 in *Mrs Thatcher's Economics: Her Legacy*, Heinemann Educational, 2nd edn, 1992.

Willets, D., Chapters 6 and 9 in *Modern Conservatism*, Penguin, 1992.

Essay topics

1. Define a market and explain why markets can improve economic welfare. Discuss how the Single European Market is intended to increase the economic welfare of member states. (Joint Matriculation Board, 1992)
2. How might privatization policies be used to increase competition and reduce monopoly? Discuss whether the UK privatization programme is likely to achieve this result. (Associated Examining Board, 1991)
3. (a) Distinguish between voluntary and involuntary unemployment.
   (b) Analyse the effects of supply side policies on both of these types of unemployment. (University of London Examinations and Assessment Council, 1990)
4. To what extent is unemployment the result of real wages being too high? (University of Oxford Delegacy of Local Examinations, 1991)

Data Response Question 4

The American experience

This task is based on a question set by the Associated Examining Board in 1991. Read the passage, which is extracted from an article entitled 'Supply side economics: an assessment of the American experience in the 1980s' by P.C. Roberts (*National Westminster Bank Quarterly Review*, 1989), and answer the following questions.

1. What is meant by the following: (i) 'to balance the budget' and (ii) 'worsening "Phillips curve" trade-offs between inflation and unemployment'.
2. Explain why the writer argues that 'supply side policy is an anti-inflationary one, because its goal is to increase real output relative to demand'.
3. Examine the view put forward by some supply side economists, that a cut in tax rates will not necessarily result in a fall in tax revenue.
4. Contrast Keynesian and supply side economists' views of the way in which fiscal policy might be used to influence the level of national output and employment.

The supply side policy in the United States was not designed to secure more revenues for the government or to balance the budget. It was directed toward overcoming the economy's inability to grow without rising inflation and toward reversing the decline in the competitive position of the United States. During the 1970s productivity growth declined sharply. Policy-makers were confronted with worsening 'Phillips curve' trade-offs between inflation and unemployment, ending in both rising inflation and unemployment. In 1971 the US merchandise trade deficit turned negative and grew dramatically during the latter part of the decade despite the continuous fall in the dollar exchange rate.

Keynesian economists could not explain these developments or offer elected policy-makers an escape from the problems. This failure created an opportunity for supply side economics, which argued that the policy of pumping up demand while neglecting incentives to produce had resulted in stagflation. As incentives were eroded, each additional increment of demand called forth less real output and more inflation. Supply-siders argued that improved incentives and less costs imposed by government would result in greater supply and more efficient use of productive inputs. The supply side policy is an anti-inflationary one, because its goal is to increase real output relative to demand.

In the Keynesian approach, a fiscal change operates to alter demand in the economy. A tax rate reduction, for example, raises the disposable income of consumers. With government spending held constant, the increased consumer spending stimulates supply and moves the economy to higher levels of employment and gross national product. In this view, the size of the deficit determines the amount of the stimulus.

In contrast, supply side economics emphasises that fiscal policy works by changing relative prices or incentives. High income tax rates and regulation are seen as disincentives to work and production regardless of the level of demand. As people respond to the higher after tax income and wealth, or greater profitability, incomes rise and the tax base grows, thus feeding back some of the lost revenues to the Treasury. The saving rate also rises, providing more funds for government and private borrowing.

Chapter Five

Taxation and social security

'In this world nothing can be said to be certain, except death and taxes.' Benjamin Franklin

Introduction
Changes in the inherited structure of taxes and social security have been a key theme of the post-1979 Conservative governments. As noted in Chapter 3, previous governments had tended to lay great stress on the need to fine-tune aggregate demand – that is, to maintain aggregate demand at a level which kept the economy at full employment – by altering tax rates with little regard for the indirect effects on the supply side. To the extent that other considerations were weighed in the balance, these were primarily concerned with social issues of equity and income distribution, rather than with the impact of tax and social security on the supply side of the economy. This approach was overturned by the incoming Conservative government in 1979, which pledged itself to reduce direct taxes on income and profit, preferably by first reducing government spending but, if necessary, by increasing indirect taxes on spending (e.g. VAT, customs and excise duties). In announcing his first budget, then the Chancellor of the Exchequer, Sir Geoffrey Howe, claimed:

> 'Our new economic strategy is built around our tax proposals. Income tax now takes a high proportion of even modest incomes. This gives rise to . . . the sapping of effort and initiative . . . and bears a considerable responsibility for industry's lack of competitiveness.'

The effect of taxes on incentives
The effect of taxes on the incentive to work can be easily analysed using the simple tools of microeconomics. *The important point in analysing the supply of labour is to recognize that the decision by a worker to supply work is equivalent to the decision to give up leisure.* Thus, the appropriate analysis is to consider the choice between income and leisure – every hour of leisure taken is an hour of income sacrificed.

The simplest case is illustrated in Figure 19. The indifference curve shown represents the combinations of income and leisure between which the individual is indifferent. Higher indifference curves would reflect higher levels of utility or welfare. The budget line indicates that a maximum of L hours of leisure can be taken per period (168 per week). If all of these hours were instead worked, then disposable income would be Y (the hourly wage rate net of tax multiplied by 168 hours). Thus, the slope of the budget line YL is the net wage rate. To maximize welfare, the individual will therefore choose the combination of income and leisure at which the highest attainable indifference curve is just tangential to the budget line. In Figure 19 this is at point E_0, which is associated with an income Y_0 and work hours $L-L_0$ (*note that hours of work are measured to the left from L*).

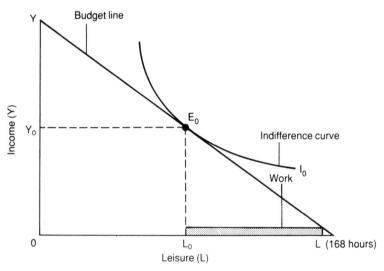

Figure 19 Analysis of the incentive to work or to have leisure

Clearly, any change in the tax rate will alter the slope of the budget line YL. Suppose, for example, that the government reduces the rate of tax (see Figure 20). The budget line would become steeper, since by working all the hours available, the individual can now earn an income Y' rather than Y. In other words, the new budget line, Y'L, now has a greater slope. Equilibrium will be achieved at point E', which is on a higher indifference curve than before, indicating an increase in the individual's welfare. But while a tax reduction unambiguously increases welfare, does it lead to an increase in the number of hours worked?

In fact, there are two effects involved. The first is the **substitution effect**. Because the tax reduction has altered the relative 'price' of leisure *vis-à-vis* work, increasing the opportunity cost of leisure in terms of income foregone, the individual will tend to substitute work for leisure. The second is the **income effect**. Because a given number of hours work now yields a higher disposable income, the individual can effectively have more of both income and leisure than before, by working fewer hours (at a higher, post-tax rate) for a higher income.

The impact of the two effects on hours worked can be disentangled in the following way. First, consider the combination of leisure and income that the individual would choose, facing the new trade-off between the two – that is, a budget constraint of slope Y'L. By drawing a pecked construction line Ce parallel to Y'L, the gain in income can be eliminated. Where Ce is tangential to the original indifference curve, at e, shows a substitution from E_0 giving the same satisfaction as at E_0 because it is on the same original indifference curve. Under such circumstances, the individual would choose a leisure–income combination of L_S and Y_S. The difference between the number of hours worked before, $L–L_0$, and the number worked due to the tax reduction ignoring the income effect, $L–L_S$, is $L_0–L_S$. This is a measure of the substitution effect. Following the tax cut, the substitution effect is positive.

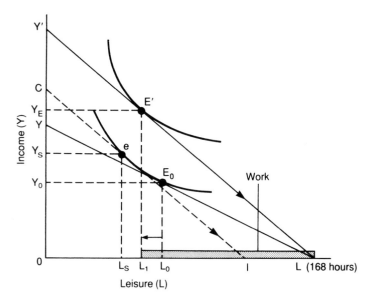

Figure 20 The effect of a cut in the tax rate; more hours worked

The rest of the change in the number of hours worked must be due to the income effect. In this case, while the substitution effect alone would have increased the number of hours worked from $L-L_0$ to $L-L_S$, the overall increase is only from $L-L_0$ to $L-L_1$. In other words, the income effect reduces the number of hours worked by L_1-L_S, confirming that it is negative. In general, therefore, following a reduction in the rate of tax, basic economic theory suggests that there will be a positive substitution effect, causing people to work more hours, and a negative income effect, encouraging people to work fewer hours. Notice that there is nothing inherent in the theory we have reviewed to suggest that the (positive) substitution effect will always outweigh the (negative) income effect. Figure 21 illustrates an equally plausible outcome. Here the reduction in the tax rate results in a positive substitution effect, L_0-L_S, which is insufficient to compensate the negative income effect, resulting in a fall in the number of hours worked, from $L-L_0$ to L_0-L_1. *Thus, it is theoretically possible that, far from strengthening the supply side in the sense of increasing the incentive to work, tax cuts may actually reduce the supply of labour.*

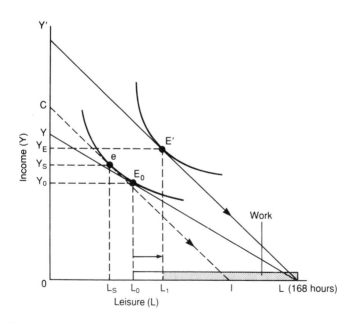

Figure 21 A cut in tax rate reducing the number of hours worked (cf. Figure 20)

Basic economic theory therefore suggests that, provided the substitution effect outweighs the income effect, tax cuts will tend to increase the incentive to work, while reductions in unemployment-related benefits (which can be thought of as negative taxes in this context) will have a similarly beneficial effect on the labour supply. There are, however, two important qualifications to this simple account. The first is *microeconomic* – most people have limited discretion over the number of hours they elect to work. The second objection is *macroeconomic* – while tax and social security cuts may stimulate an increase in the number of people wanting to work, unless macroeconomic conditions are such that there are jobs available, the increase in employment and output will fail to materialize.

The Laffer curve

Arguing that tax and social security cuts are necessary to strengthen the supply side of the economy poses an awkward policy problem. Because the number of unemployed drawing social security is small relative to the number of taxpayers, any concerted supply side initiative is likely to result in much deeper falls in tax revenues than there are offsetting savings in social security outlays. However, in the mid-1970s Professor Arthur Laffer offered a solution to this apparent conflict between supply side objectives and prudent fiscal policy. He pointed out that there is logically a direct relationship between the rate of taxation and the amount of revenue raised (see Figure 22). At a tax rate of 0 per cent, revenue will clearly be zero. At a tax rate of 100 per cent, revenue will also be zero since there is no incentive to work in a taxable activity. Between these two extremes, therefore, there will be a function relating the amount of tax revenues to the tax rate which will be initially positive, at some point reaching a maximum (in this case at tax rate T_0). before falling back to zero. In other words, the tax revenue function will follow the bell shape of the so-called 'Laffer curve'.

Laffer was not the first to spot this relationship, as the following quotation from Adam Smith's *The Wealth of Nations* suggests:

> 'High taxes, sometimes by diminishing the consumption of the taxed commodities, and sometimes by encouraging smuggling, frequently afford a smaller revenue than what might be drawn from more moderate taxes.'

Laffer's contribution, however, was to provide an alternative explanation for a possible inverse relationship between tax rates and tax revenue, based on the effects on high taxes on the incentive to produce, rather than their tendency to depress consumption or encourage dishonest tax evasion. It struck a sympathetic chord with many new

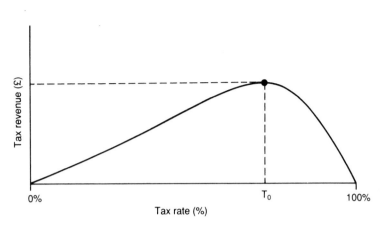

Figure 22 The Laffer curve

classical economists, who saw that, provided the government inherits tax rates that are above T_0 in Figure 22, it need not delay tax cuts for fear of running a budget deficit. This is because a cut in tax rates will not only stimulate the supply side of the economy, but – by more than proportionately boosting income – also increase tax revenue. It was the belief that US tax rates (which were incidentally much lower than those then prevailing in Europe) were above T_0 that encouraged the incoming Reagan administration to cut income tax heavily between 1981 and 1983 in the USA. In the event, a huge budget deficit emerged, although supporters of the tax cuts argue that this was primarily the result of a failure to control federal spending during the 1980s, rather than the depressing effect of the tax cuts on federal revenue.

In the UK, for certain sectors of the population, it was generally recognized that tax rates were above T_0. In 1979, for example, the top **marginal rate of income tax** was a staggering 98 per cent – comprising a tax rate of 83 per cent, plus a 15 per cent 'unearned' income surcharge for income derived from, for example, shares or property. Unsurprisingly, many wealthy individuals chose to live abroad as 'tax exiles', rather than pay such penal rates. Significantly, as the top rates of tax have fallen below those in continental Europe, the phenomenon of rock stars commuting to London from their homes in Switzerland had ended and the share of tax revenues collected from the richest 5 per cent of the population has increased – as the Laffer curve predicts.

For the vast majority of tax payers, however, the Conservative government was unconvinced by the argument that tax rates were above T_0 and tax cuts for average earners have been introduced slowly over successive parliaments, with the Treasury reducing taxes by only what its present finances would allow, rather than risking deeper cuts in the hope of a spontaneous, supply side induced increase in income and tax revenues.

Tax policy, 1979–92

Between 1979 and 1992, Conservative governments introduced fourteen Budgets, thirteen of which involved significant reductions in direct taxes (the exception was in 1981). As we have seen, the net incentive effect of tax cuts on households depends upon the size of the (positive) substitution effect, and the size of the (negative) income effect. In the simple examples used to illustrate this point above, we made no distinction between the marginal rate of tax (the proportion of any increase in income paid in tax) and the **average rate of tax** (proportion of total income paid in tax). *Indeed, with a straight-line budget constraint, they are the same thing.* In the real world, however, the two may differ markedly. In most countries the actual tax system is 'progressive', with marginal rates that increase with income, giving rise to a variable average tax rate.

Consider the following simplified example of the structure facing a typical income-earner: there is a tax-free allowance of £5000 pa; between £5001 and £10 000 the marginal rate of tax is 20 per cent, rising to 30 per cent between £10 001 and £15 000, 40 per cent between £15 001 and £20 000 and 50 per cent thereafter. Table 10 shows the marginal and average tax rates at different levels of income. Only in the tax-free band and at infinitely high incomes are the two the same, with the average rate of tax rising continuously from 0 per cent towards 50 per cent once the taxable threshold is crossed.

Table 10 Marginal and average tax rate

Pre-tax income	Marginal rate of tax	Tax paid	Average rate of tax
£5000	0%	£0	0%
£10 000	20%	£1000	10%
£15 000	30%	£2500	16.7%
£20 000	40%	£4500	22.5%
£25 000	50%	£7000	28%
£50 000	50%	£19 500	39%
£5 000 000	50%	£2 494 500	49.9%

The significance of marginal and average tax rates is that it is the former which determines the size of the substitution effect and the latter which determines the income effect. To maximize the impact on the supply of labour, tax reform should aim to reduce marginal rates of tax (which causes individuals to substitute work for leisure), while changing the tax structure to moderate the fall in the average tax rate (which discourages work effort, by leaving individuals with more of their post-tax income). In the scenario above, for example, we can see that a worker earning £50 000 pa is subject to a marginal tax rate of 50 per cent, but an average tax rate of 39 per cent. By cutting the marginal tax rate to 45 per cent and abolishing the £5000 tax-free allowance (so that the first £5000 of income is now taxed at 20 per cent, the next £5000 at 30 per cent, the next £5000 at 40 per cent and the remaining income at 45 per cent, rather than 50 per cent), the average tax rate for this worker would actually rise to 41 per cent – leading to both a positive substitution and a positive income effect.

Between 1979 and 1992, the marginal rate of income tax paid by top income earners was cut from 83 per cent (98 per cent for unearned income from investments) to 40 per cent, one of the lowest top rates in the European Community. The basic rate was similarly cut from an

"Er... plus VAT, sir"

inherited rate of 33 per cent to 25 per cent and all other marginal income tax rates were abolished. (although, perversely a new bottom rate of 20 per cent was introduced in 1992). The rate of VAT was sharply increased from 8 per cent in 1979 to 17.5 per cent in two jumps. Overall, therefore, it appears that the structure of income tax has become much less progressive, which may have improved incentives to work.

However, the situation is complicated by other factors. For example, employees' national insurance contributions (NICs) were increased from 6.5 per cent to 9 per cent over the same period. Since NICs are another tax, albeit one that is 'earmarked' for a specific purpose (financing social security payments to the old, sick and unemployed), this increase means that for many income taxpayers the reduction in their marginal tax rates was less than the cuts in income tax rates would suggest. Table 11 shows the combined impact of all these changes on the marginal rates of tax faced by an individual on average earnings, illustrating that the net effect has been a modest decline from 48.8 per cent to 45.9 per cent. For higher income-earners, of course, the decline has been very much sharper.

Table 11 Marginal percentage tax rates for workers on average earnings

Year	VAT*	Income tax	NICs: employee	NICs: employer	Total
1978–79	4.85	33.0	6.50	12.75	48.8
1979–80	8.25	30.0	6.50	13.50	48.3
1980–81	8.25	30.0	6.75	13.70	48.6
1981–82	8.25	30.0	7.75	13.70	49.4
1982–83	8.25	30.0	8.75	13.70	50.2
1983–84	8.25	30.0	9.00	11.95	49.7
1984–85	8.25	30.0	9.00	10.45	49.4
1985–86	8.25	30.0	9.00	10.45	49.0
1986–87	8.25	29.0	9.00	10.45	48.1
1987–88	8.25	27.0	9.00	10.45	46.5
1988–89	8.25	25.0	9.00	10.45	44.5
1989–90	8.25	25.0	9.00	10.45	44.5
1990–91	8.25	25.0	9.00	10.45	44.5
1991–92	9.65	25.0	9.00	10.45	45.9
1992–93	9.65	25.0	9.00	10.45	45.9

*VAT rate is calculated from the proportion of consumer goods which carry VAT, multiplied by the prevailing VAT rate.

While the marginal rates of tax faced by workers have fallen since 1979, despite political rhetoric to the contrary (in line with the government's declared commitment to reduce the burden of taxation), the average rate of tax has actually increased slightly. This has been primarily due to 'fiscal drag', the process by which the average tax burden automatically rises during a period of economic growth. Under the so-called 'Rooker–Wise' amendment, tax allowances and bands in Britain are indexed to the retail price index (i.e. they are raised at each Budget in line with inflation). They are not increased, however, as real incomes grow (refer back to Table 10). We can see that, if (at constant prices) average earnings in 1979 had been £10 000, the average tax rate would have been 10 per cent. Real income growth of roughly 3 per cent a year would have increased average earnings to £15 000 by 1992. Without any change to the tax structure, the average tax rate would have automatically increased to 16.7 per cent. It is primarily through this mechanism that the average tax rate has increased slightly in Britain.

The community charge

The community charge, or 'poll tax', is worthy of mention, as it represents the high-water mark of the new classical tax revolution. In terms of its impact on incentives, a **lump-sum tax** which is unrelated to ability to pay is the ideal way of raising government revenue. For a lump-sum tax the marginal rate of tax is 0 per cent, hence it creates no disincentive to work. In April 1990, the Conservative government replaced the former system of domestic rates – under which households had paid an annual local tax related to the value of their housing (and hence, indirectly, to their wealth and income) – with a lump-sum community charge. Each adult within a council district was required to pay the same amount, although there was some help for the poorest individuals through the social security system.

Regardless of its elegance in supply side terms, however, the community charge violated an important principle of taxation, namely that the system be perceived as **equitable**. In the event, the notion that a duke should pay the same local tax as his chauffeur led to a massive, and at times violent, public outcry against the system. The government quickly backed down. In the 1991 Budget, the average community charge was reduced by £140 per person by raising VAT to 17.5 per cent to compensate for the loss of revenue, and in April 1993 a new **council tax** is scheduled to replace the community charge. Like the rates, the council tax will be related to the value of the individual's property. The public rejection of the community charge highlights the political difficulties of supply side reform in the motive area of personal taxation.

The reform of social security

Social security benefits also affect incentives to work, creating – through their interaction with the tax system – anomalies such as the **unemployment trap** and the **poverty trap**. The unemployment trap refers to the situation in which an individual finds, owing to the payment of taxes on earned income and the withdrawal of benefits, that he or she has a higher disposable income when unemployed than if he or she worked. In other words, there is a positive financial disincentive to seek work.

The extent of this disincentive is captured by the so-called **replacement ratio**, defined as the ratio of total benefits while unemployed to disposable income while in work. For an unskilled worker with a dependent partner and school-aged children, total unemployment-related benefits may be high relative to the disposable income that could be expected from work, resulting in a replacement ratio which may be close to, or even above, unity. For example, imagine that weekly benefits while unemployed are £100. If the highest wage that the worker can command, net of tax, is only £120, then the replacement ratio is 100/120, or 84 per cent. When replacement ratios are high, it is easy to see why people may be deterred from working, thereby reducing the supply of labour and weakening the supply side of the economy. In our example, the unfortunate individual is effectively being invited to work for a mere £20 a week, so it would hardly be surprising if he or she chose leisure over full-time employment.

The poverty trap is closely related to the unemployment trap, operating in a similar way for individuals on low incomes. Because low earnings are supplemented by means-tested, or income-related, benefits (e.g. free school meals, free health care, welfare payments), a badly-designed system can penalize workers who take higher-paying jobs twice over: first, by denying them continued access to a means-tested benefit they previously enjoyed; and secondly, by taxing the extra income at an increasing marginal rate. In extreme cases, the overall effect can be to reduce disposable income (including non-monetary benefits), so deterring workers from seeking better-paid positions.

Corporation tax reforms

In addition to changes in income tax, Conservative government has also introduced changes in the structure and level of corporation tax. In the 1984 Budget, the main rate of corporation tax was reduced in stages from 52 per cent to 35 per cent by the end of 1986–87, while capital allowances (i.e. capital spending that could be offset against gross profits for tax purposes) of 100 per cent for plant and machinery and of 75 per cent for industrial buildings were phased out over a three-year period and replaced by a less generous system of tax allowances. So-called 'stock relief', which permitted companies to exclude increases in the value of their stocks due to inflation (which would otherwise have the effect of increasing their taxable profits), was abolished.

The logic of these changes was to remove 'distortions' from the corporate tax system which, it was argued, encouraged companies to plough capital into projects that were only 'profitable' because of the favourable tax treatment they attracted. The introduction of a level playing field, in which companies could appraise all investments on the same footing, free from government interference, was accompanied by a significant reduction in the rate of corporation tax, leaving companies with a larger share of their gross profits. These reforms were reinforced by the 1991 Budget, which further reduced the rate of corporation tax from 35 per cent to 33 per cent over a two-year period.

Conclusions

Since 1979, Conservative governments have stressed the role of tax and social security reform in order to promote incentives to work and invest. This emphasis is, of course, partly derived from wider political objectives of promoting individual freedom and responsibility, rather than allowing people to rely passively on a paternalist welfare state. Nevertheless, the government has expected major economic dividends from restructuring of taxes and social security in terms of a revitalized supply side.

We have seen that economic theory suggests that such reforms, by altering the opportunity cost of leisure, can have two, offsetting effects: a positive substitution effect, whereby workers substitute work for leisure; and a negative income effect. Whether tax and social security reforms are successful depends, in part, upon which of these two effects is the stronger. Theory does indicate, however, that it is marginal rates of tax which are most relevant for determining the size of the substitution effect and average rates of income tax that primarily determine the size of the income effect. To the extent that the reforms introduced by Conservative governments have reduced marginal rates of tax, without having much impact on the overall burden of taxation, they have probably had a positive effect on incentives.

KEY WORDS

Substitution effect   Equitable
Income effect   Council tax
Laffer curve   Unemployment trap
Marginal rate of income tax   Poverty trap
Average rate of tax   Replacement ratio
Lump sum tax

Reading list

Maunders, P., et al, Chapter 20 in *Economics Explained*, Collins Educational, 2nd edn, 1991.

Richards, K., 'Redistribution under Conservatism: past and future', in N. Healey (ed.), *Britain's Economic 'Miracle': Myth or Reality?*, Routledge, 1992.

Robins, P., 'Government policy, taxation and supply side economics', in N. Healey (ed.), *Britain's Economic 'Miracle': Myth or Reality?* Routledge, 1992.

Smith, D., Chapter 4 in *Mrs Thatcher's Economics: Her Legacy*, 2nd edn, Heinemann Educational, 1992.

Whynes, D., Chapter 3 in *Welfare State Economics*, Heinemann Educational, 1992.

Wilkinson, M., Chapter 7 in *Equity and Efficiency*, Heinemann Educational, 1993.

Essay topics

1. What factors determine the level of aggregate supply in the economy? Explain how reductions in taxation might be used to increase aggregate supply and discuss how successful such a policy is likely to be. (Joint Matriculation Board, 1990)

2. 'The Conservative government's consistent aim has been to bring down the tax burden when it is prudent to do so, and in particular to reduce the basic rate of income tax. Progress has been considerable' (Conservative Party Campaign Guide, April 1991). Discuss. (Oxford & Cambridge Schools Examination Board, 1992)

3. In 1978 the standard rate of income tax in the UK was 33 per cent and the top rate was 83 per cent; in 1990 the standard rate was 25 per cent and the top rate was 40 per cent. Examine the likely economic consequences of these changes. (University of London Examinations and Assessment Council, 1992)

4. (a) Explain why the effect of a price change (other things being equal) on the quantity of a good demanded by a consumer can be conceptually broken down into an 'income effect' and a 'substitution effect'. Illustrate these two effects diagrammatically in the case of a price fall of a 'normal' good.

(b) It has often been observed that as some individuals' real wage rates increase, they prefer to work for shorter hours. Explain how this observation can be viewed as the product of an income effect offsetting a substitution effect. (In this context an individual can be regarded as choosing between two 'commodities', leisure and money income, the appropriate relative price being the wage rate.) (Welsh Joint Education Committee, 1991)

5. 'The United Kingdom's taxation and welfare benefits systems have trapped the low-waged in relative poverty and the un-waged in unemployment.' (a) Explain the causes of this situation. (b) Explain how problems created by this situation might be reduced. (Associated Examination Board, 1991)

Data Response Question 5

Taxation
This task is based on a question set by the University of London Examinations & Assessment Council in 1990. Study Tables A and B which show changes in the taxation of the incomes of married couples between 1987–88 and 1988–89. It is assumed that only the husband has earned income.

Table A Marginal rates of income tax

1987/88		1988/89	
Slice of taxable income (£)	Marginal rate of tax (%)	Slice of taxable income (£)	Marginal rate of tax (%)
1–17,900	27	1–19,300	25
17,901–20,400	40	Over 19,300	40
20,401–25,400	45		
25,401–33,300	50		
33,301–41,200	55		
Over 41,200	60		

(Source: *The Financial Times* 16 March 1988.)

Table B Average rates of income tax

Charge for 1987–88			Charge for 1988–89		Reduction in tax after change	
Income	Income tax (£)	% of total income in tax	Income tax (£)	% of total income in tax	Income tax (£)	As a % of total income
4,000	55	1,4	0	0	55	1,3
5,000	325	6,5	226	4,5	99	1,9
6,000	595	9,9	476	7,9	119	1,9
7,000	865	12,4	726	10,3	139	1,9
8,000	1,135	14,2	976	12,2	159	1,9
9,000	1,405	15,6	1,226	13,6	179	1,9
10,000	1,675	16,8	1,476	14,7	199	1,9
12,000	2,215	18,5	1,976	16,4	239	1,9
14,000	2,755	19,7	2,476	17,6	279	1,9
16,000	3,295	20,6	2,976	18,6	319	1,9
18,000	3,835	21,3	3,476	19,3	359	1,9
20,000	4,375	21,9	3,976	19,8	399	1,9
25,000	6,195	24,8	5,467	21,8	728	2,9
30,000	8,486	28,3	7,467	24,9	1,019	3,3
40,000	13,631	34,1	11,467	28,6	2,164	5,4
50,000	19,381	38,8	15,467	30,9	3,914	7,8
60,000	25,381	42,3	19,467	32,4	5,914	9,8
70,000	31,381	44,8	23,467	33,5	7,914	11,3

(Source: *The Times,* 16 March 1988.)

1. With reference to Table A define the meaning of the term 'marginal rate of tax'.
2. Describe the main changes in marginal tax rates between 1987–88 and 1988–89.
3. With reference to Tables A and B, explain the relationship between marginal and average tax rates in 1988–89.
4. Using economic analysis, examine the possible effects of the changes in marginal tax rates on: (i) incentives to work, (ii) tax revenues, (iii) the level of economic activity.

Chapter Six

Labour market reform

*'For many years, the UK's economic performance has been hindered
by rigidities in the labour market, by unwillingness to accept change
and by unrealistic attitudes to pay and performance.'*
HM Treasury, 1986

A central plank of the post-1979 Conservative governments' supply
side programme has been the reform of the labour market. It is important to note that many of the tax and social security policies were
intended to work through the labour market: reductions in employers'
National Insurance contributions (NICs) reduce the cost of labour to
employers, encouraging them to expand employment and thus increasing the natural rate of output; income tax cuts and reductions in social
security benefits increase the incentive to work, thereby increasing the
supply of labour at any given wage rate and so increasing the natural
rate of output. The labour market reforms discussed in this chapter,
however, relate to measures that impact directly on the labour market
in the first instance – for example, changes to the laws on **collective
wage bargaining** by trades unions.

Trade unions and the supply side
The Conservative government charges trade unions with inhibiting the
flexible operation of the labour market by preventing necessary downwards adjustments in wages and thereby prolonging the period during
which deflationary shocks to the economy depress output below its
natural rate – and correspondingly push unemployment above its natural rate. In other words, in terms of the aggregate supply and demand
(AS–AD) model, trade unions are accused of extending the length of the
short run, by slowing down the speed with which wages and prices
adjust to slumps in AD so that the economy returns to its natural rate of
output more slowly than would otherwise be the case.

*Introducing the role of trade unions into the AS–AD model in this
way suggests there is likely to be an important asymmetry in the way
the economy adjusts to changes in AD.* Following a fall in AD, rational
behaviour by monopolistic trade unions will tend to drag out the

adjustment process, extending the period during which the economy languishes below its natural rate of output. Conversely, an increase in AD is likely to have only a transitory effect on output and employment as trade unions immediately seek to bargain for wage increases to compensate for any rise in prices. The implication is that, by distorting the functioning of the supply side in this fashion, the presence of trade unions will tend to lower the average long-run rate of output and raise the average long-run rate of unemployment. This is because cyclical fluctuations in AD will boost prices and wages, rather than output and employment, in an upswing, but depress output below its natural rate and increase unemployment in recession, having only a muted effect on prices and wages.

Trade unions and economic growth

In addition to distorting the smooth functioning of the supply side in this asymmetric way, the Conservative government also accuses trade unions of inhibiting private sector research and development (R&D) and investment in physical and human capital. The trade union movement in the UK has historically been 'craft-based', with workers joining unions that cover their particular occupation (e.g. printing or engineering). The monopoly power of an individual trade union thus resides in its power to control labour of a specific functional type. For example, a nationally based engineering union can bargain with employers from a very powerful base, since companies will find it very difficult to recruit qualified engineering workers who are not union members.

One potential disadvantage of this union structure is that it may militate against supply side change. R&D and investment strengthen the economy by improving productivity; that is, by changing the way that people work and thereby increasing output per head. For example, the computerization of newspaper typesetting, which allows journalists to type their stories into a computer that automatically sets up the printing presses, was a great advance over the old system, which required print workers manually to assemble plates of individual letters from the journalists' draft typescript. This technological innovation dramatically improved both labour productivity and technical quality in the newspaper industry, but by fundamentally altering the functional nature of the jobs involved, its introduction proved very disruptive, culminating in the protracted and bitter 'Wapping' dispute between the print workers' unions and the Murdoch newspaper company.

Part of the difficulty stemmed from the fact that the computerization of the printsetting operation in the newspaper business transformed what had been a manual job done by skilled printer workers – repre-

"And now the BBC takes a long cool look at the scandal of over-manning and restrictive practices in British Industry"

sented by their own craft union – into a job which could be done directly by journalists, supported by electrical engineers to maintain the new equipment. The print workers' union was thus bound to defend the position of its members against the effects of the changes which, given the intransigence of the employer concerned, resulted in prolonged strike action. The Conservative government's argument is, therefore, that since economic growth necessarily involves continuously redefining workers' jobs and functional responsibilities, old craft-based trade unions which have a duty to protect the jobs of their membership from structural change inhibit R&D and investment in new products and processes. Trade unions retort that, provided employers are prepared to retrain and upgrade the skills of their existing workforce, rather than discard them in favour of better qualified outsiders whenever job specifications change, there need be no conflict between job security and structural change. Whatever the rights and wrongs of this ongoing debate, it is the government's concern that unions may retard economic change that has provided the second rationale of its reform of the labour market.

Trade union legislation
Since 1979, a series of statutes has placed restrictions on trade union activity, in order, according to a Treasury statement in 1986, to:

'reduce the monopoly power of the trade unions . . . (and so) create a climate in which realistic pay bargaining and acceptance of flexible working practices become the norm.'

The government has targeted two aspects of trade unions in particular: first, their ability to undertake strike action, and secondly, their right to enforce a **closed shop** (an arrangement whereby all employees within a company must belong to a recognized trade union). For example:

- The 1980 Employment Act made secondary picketing illegal.
- The 1982 Employment Act specified that a lawful trade dispute must 'wholly or mainly' relate to employment matters, in an attempt to prevent political strikes.
- The 1984 Trade Union Act required industrial action to be formally approved in advance by the union members concerned in a secret ballot.
- The 1988 Employment Act gave union members the right not to be disciplined by their union for failing to take part in industrial action, further weakening a union's ability to mobilize an effective strike.
- Finally, the 1990 Employment Act made it unlawful to deny people a job on the grounds that they are not union members.

The results of this legislative onslaught on the trade union movement have been profound. Although it is difficult to disentangle the effects of the new laws (which have tended to reduce the benefits of union membership) from those resulting from structural economic change (which have altered the composition of the employed labour force, creating female, part-time jobs at the expense of traditional, full-time manual employment), the fact remains that between 1979 and 1992 union density fell dramatically (see Figure 23). (Union density is defined as the percentage of employed workers eligible for membership of a trade union who actually exercise this right and join a union.) Although Conservative governments have never suggested that they actively sought this outcome, the decline in union membership has nevertheless been at least partially influenced by the more hostile legislative environment and has played a major part in altering the balance of power in the industrial relations arena.

A less controversial indicator of the success of the government's new legal framework for wage bargaining has been the marked fall in the number of days lost through industrial disputes (see Figure 24). Although there was a sudden surge in days lost during the protracted and highly divisive miners' strike of 1984–85, the underlying trend since 1979 appears to have been firmly downwards.

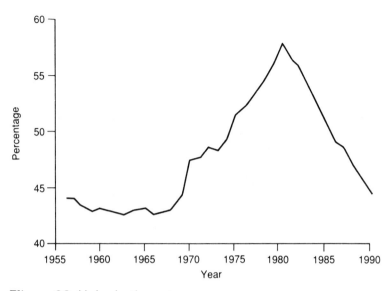

Figure 23 Unionization rate

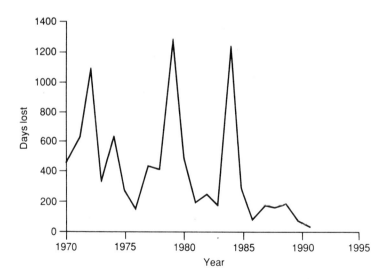

Figure 24 Industrial disputes: days lost per thousand people in employment

Labour mobility and the natural rate of unemployment

In addition to reducing the monopoly power of trade unions and removing legislative obstacles, the objective of 'improving the flexibility of the labour market' has also included measures to promote both occupational and geographical **labour mobility**. These policies have been inspired by the apparent increase in the **natural rate of unemployment** in the economy over the last 20 years. As we saw in Chapter 2, the natural rate of unemployment is the rate of unemployment consistent with equilibrium in the labour market; that is, with the supply of labour equal to the demand for labour. But if supply equals demand, how can there be any unemployment? In the real world, of course, the answer depends upon the way in which the government chooses to officially record unemployment. When the labour market is in equilibrium, there are millions of adults who, for whatever reason, choose not to seek work at the equilibrium wage rate. Are they unemployed? For example, is a trained solicitor who looks after her children at home unemployed? Is a male accountant who takes early retirement at fifty unemployed? In principle, although neither wants a job at the going wage rate, each may begin looking (and regard her- or himself as unemployed) if wages were higher. Clearly, the actual definition of unemployment is problematic.

However, in terms of our simple labour supply and demand model, our definition of the natural rate of unemployment excludes workers who are **voluntarily unemployed**. It refers to those workers who, in equilibrium, are simply moving between jobs; that is, leaving one job to go to another. Equilibrium in the labour market means that the number of jobs being offered by employers (actual jobs filled plus unfilled vacancies) equals the number of jobs demanded by workers (jobs taken plus unemployed seeking jobs). Labour market equilibrium is thus consistent with the idea of some minimum level of unemployment, as workers leave one job and go to another. As they move, they fill one vacancy and, in moving, create another. If the workforce is 25 million and each person takes one week to move jobs once a year, then on the average, at any moment in time 0.5 million people will be temporarily unemployed even though the labour market overall is in full equilibrium.

It follows that the more difficult it is for people to move smoothly between jobs, either because their skills do not match up precisely with the jobs on offer or because they live in a different part of the country from the location of the new jobs, the longer that workers are temporarily unemployed while switching jobs. If, in our example, each worker was unemployed for four weeks, there would on average be 2 million unemployed at any moment in time. In the UK the pace of structural change in the economy has recently been so rapid with manufacturing shedding labour faster than the expanding service sector can take up the slack, that the number of unemployed consistent with labour market equilibrium (i.e. the natural rate of unemployment) rose in the 1970s and early 1980s (Figure 25). The government has accordingly laid great emphasis on the need to promote occupational and geographical labour mobility in an effort to bring down the natural rate of unemployment.

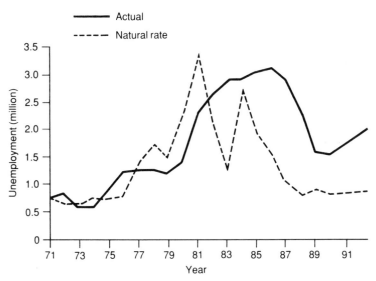

Figure 25 Unemployment trends

Occupational mobility

Although there are sound supply side reasons for investing resources in the training and education of all workers – in order to improve their productivity – the government's training policies have been primarily directed at the long-term unemployed, with the aim of equipping the unemployed with the appropriate skills they need to find work. Youth Training Schemes and Job Training Schemes for young workers date back to the early 1980s. 'Restart' and similar training and reskilling programmes targeted at the unemployed, with varying degrees of success, have also proved a major element in the government's response to persistent mismatches of supply and demand in the labour market.

Geographical mobility

One of the major impediments to job mobility from the northern regions of high unemployment to the relatively more prosperous South East of England is the higher cost of private housing in the South. Approximately 70 per cent of families now live in their own homes, forcing them to buy and sell if they are to take jobs in other regions. Although the slump in the housing market since 1988 has hit the South East hardest, reducing the size of the 'north-south' price differential, house prices in the South East still remain an average of 50 per cent higher than those in the northern regions. For those in rented accommodation, long waiting lists make it very difficult to obtain council housing in a new area. The setting up of a Tenants' Exchange Scheme and a National Mobility Office are designed to assist geographical mobility, but it remains restricted owing to high house prices in the South East, cuts in local authority housing programmes and the continued absence of a significant private rented sector.

Conclusions

A flexible, efficient labour force is clearly crucial for a successful supply side. There is little doubt that, before 1979, the British labour market was excessively rigid and plagued by poor industrial relations. The trade union reforms undertaken by Conservative governments, initially against strong opposition from the labour movement, have proved electorally popular. While the government may yet sign up for the EC's Social Chapter sometime in the future, extending trade union powers in certain limited areas, it seems likely that the balance of industrial power between employers and unions has changed permanently.

In other respects, Conservative governments have introduced useful schemes to promote occupational and geographical mobility, aimed at reducing the natural rate of unemployment, but these have been modest. Moreover, the data presented in Chapter 2 on skill shortages and the poor standard of training and education suggest that the UK still faces serious, and as yet unresolved, problems in terms of the quality of its labour force.

KEY WORDS

Collective wage bargaining	Labour mobility
Closed shop	Natural rate of unemployment
Secret ballot	Voluntarily unemployed

Reading list

Clark, A. and Layard R., *UK Unemployment*, 2nd edn, Heinemann Educational, 1992.

Gavin, M. and Swann, P., 'The minimum wage debate?', *Economic Review*, 1992, vol. 9(3), pp. 2–6.

Minford, P., 'Better news from the trenches: the UK labour market and the supply-side', in G. Keating, et al, *The State of the Economy: 1992*, Institute of Economic Affairs, 1992.

Simpson, L. and Paterson, I., 'Economics of trade union power', in Healey, N. (ed), *Britain's Economic Miracle: Myth or Reality?* Routledge, 1992.

Smith, D., Chapter 6 in *Mrs Thatcher's Economics: Her Legacy*, Heinemann Educational, 2nd edn, 1992.

Wilkinson, M., Chapter 8 in *Equity and Efficiency*, Heinemann Educational, 1993.

Essay topics

1. What factors are likely to determine the relative strength of trade union bargaining power in the cases of agriculture workers, ambulance workers, school teachers and electricity supply workers? Discuss whether or not it is likely that trade unions can improve the level of wages in an industry or occupation beyond what the level would be in a free market. (Joint Matriculation Board, 1990)

2. What factors contribute to the immobility of labour in the UK? How effective have government policies been since 1979 in improving the mobility of labour? (Joint Matriculation Board, A/S Level, 1992)

3. Outline how trade unions may influence the supply of labour. Examine the extent to which a significant reduction in the power of trade unions would (i) make the wage structure more flexible, and (ii) improve long term living standards. (University of London Examinations and Assessment Council, 1991)

4. What have been the main changes in trade unions in the last decade? Why are there signs of recovery now? (Oxford & Cambridge Schools Examinations Board, 1990)

5. What economic effects may trade unions have on the wages and employment of: (a) their own members; (b) non-unionised workers? Can the actions of trade unions raise the rate of inflation? (University of Oxford Delegacy of Local Examinations, 1992)

Data Response Question 6

Trade unions in the UK
This task is based on a question set by the Oxford & Cambridge
Schools Examination Board in 1992. Study Table A and answer the
questions.

Table A Trade unions

Year	Number of unions at end of year	Total union membership (thousands)	Number of industrial stoppages	Working days lost in industrial stoppages (thousands)
1979	453	13 289	2 125	29 474
1980	438	12 947	1 348	11 964
1981	414	12 106	1 344	4 266
1982	408	11 593	1 538	5 313
1983	394	11 236	1 364	3 754
1984	375	10 994	1 221	27 135
1985	370	10 821	903	6 402
1986	335	10 539	1 074	1 920
1987	330	10 475	1 016	3 546
1988	315	10 376	781	3 702
1989	309	10 158	701	4 128
1990	301*	9 940*	630	1 903

*Estimates.
Source: *Employment Gazette,* June and July 1991; *ACAS Annual Report*

1. Account for the decline in the number of unions and in total union
   membership between 1979 and 1990.
2. Account for the decline in industrial stoppages and in working days
   lost between 1979 and 1990.
3. Can it be concluded that trade union power is now no longer of
   importance?

Concluding remarks

'Supply side economics [is] common sense ... Economists have long recognised the importance of an economy's productive capacity – its stock of labour and capital and the incentives needed to get the best out of them ... Marx was in many respects a supply side economist.'
The Economist

There is nothing new about 'supply side economics'. Although the term came into common usage only relatively recently, the idea that governments should direct economic policies towards strengthening the supply side dates back to Adam Smith. Indeed, according to Colin Harbury and Richard Lipsey: 'supply side economics . . . is what Adam Smith's *Wealth of Nations* was all about'. The argument has always been over the best means to achieve the end of a vital supply side, rather than over the end itself.

Until the 1930s, governments believed that the best way to promote economic growth was to provide a stable, laissez-faire business environment in which private sector activity could flourish. During the depression of the interwar years, faith in the ability of free markets to deliver economic prosperity was badly dented. The so-called 'Keynesian revolution' overturned the apparently discredited classical orthodoxy, encouraging postwar governments to intervene directly in the supply side to achieve their objectives for growth. In recent years, however, the pendulum has come full circle, with the new classical 'counter-revolution' challenging the Keynesian approach to the supply side. Under the guidance of new classical economists, governments around the world have set about dismantling the apparatus of state regulation and control, in an attempt to breathe life back into the market forces they now charge excessive government with having suffocated.

In the UK the results of this intellectual backlash against state intervention in the supply side have been mixed. Output and productivity growth both improved in the 1980s relative to the period 1973–79, but failed to regain the momentum enjoyed during the 1960s – when Keynesianism was at its zenith. Industrial relations have undoubtedly benefited from the new legislative framework introduced by successive

Conservative governments, and strikes have fallen to record lows. On the other hand, investment in both physical and human capital (training and education) remains well below the levels taken for granted in other advanced economies, and R&D is on a downward trend.

Against this background the indications are that a process of convergence towards a more balanced approach to supply side policy is likely to prevail over the rest of this century. While new classical, free market policies have strengthened the supply side in certain areas (e.g. labour relations), the experience of the 1980s has revealed important limitations in the laissez-faire philosophy. As we saw in Chapter 3, some types of economic activity are plagued by market failure: private companies are loath to train workers, since it is more cost-effective (at the level of the individual company) to free-ride in the hope that rivals will train staff who can subsequently be poached; similarly, it is cheaper to wait for other firms to pay for pioneering R&D, producing cheaper imitation products once the new technology has been perfected. In these areas, the shift to the right in supply side policy has left the UK lagging behind our major rivals, but with the re-election of the Conservative government in 1992 for a fourth term of office and the appointment of Mr Heseltine to the Department of Trade and Industry, 'intervention is back in business'.

Reading list

Eltis, W., 'The lessons for Britain from the superior economic performance of Germany and Japan', *National Westminster Bank Quarterly Review*, 1992, Feb., pp. 2–23.

Helm, D. et al., 'Supply side policy: success or failure?', *Economic Review*, 1992, vol. 9 (4), pp. 26–28.

Essay topics

1. What are 'supply side' policies? Can such policies lead to an improvement in a country's economic performance? (Associated Examining Board, 1991)
2. 'UK Governments in the 1980s were primarily concerned about increasing incentives, generating greater competition and eliminating market imperfections.' (a) Outline the various policies which were implemented to achieve these objectives. (b) On what criteria could the effectiveness of these policies be evaluated? (University of London Examinations and Assessment Council, 1991)

Index